The Illuminati Luciferian Agenda

CHAPTER ONE

The following is a transcript of a recording distributed in 1967 by Myron C. Fagan. He had hoped that if enough Americans had heard (or read) this summary, the Illuminati's plan to destroy America would have been aborted, just as Russia's Alexander I had torpedoed the Illuminati's plans for a One World, League of Nations at the Congress of Vienna from 1814-15.

Fagan correctly describes those members of congress, the executive branch, and the judicial branch of that time as TRAITORS for their role in assisting to implement the downfall of America's sovereignty. It is the same today in 2012. It's understandable that most listeners of that period would have found it difficult to believe that the Kennedy's, for instance, were (are) part of the Illuminati plot, but he did say that JFK had a spiritual rebirth and attempted to rescue the country from the Illuminati's stranglehold by issuing US silver certificates, which apparently greatly contributed to the Illuminati's decision to assassinate him (his son, John Jr., was also murdered because he had intended to expose his father's killers after he gained public office).

Today we realize that the Illuminati exerts almost 100% control over all three branches of the American government and the few remaining congressional defenders of America can be counted on one hand as the intense public vilification and disparagement directed at then Rep. Cynthia McKinney of Georgia will bear witness to. It's too late in the game now to expect any patriot remaining within government service to rescue us from the brutal destruction that lies ahead, but the American people can save themselves from these satanic destroyers of liberty and life through NON-COOPERATION and NON-COMPLIANCE.

The Illuminati plans to incorporate MIND CONTROL to force compliance, but their ELF mind control towers can be neutralized before that happens if enough people become aware of the enslavement agenda. The current crop of traitors with names like Rumsfeld, Bush, Clinton, Obama, are merely stooges for hidden corporate Satanists who, in turn, are themselves stooges for repressive overlords as described in the latest books of David Icke and the lectures of Al Bielek. You must play some role to help save your children and this world from these madmen. Help fulfill Fagan's Hope and distribute this book far and wide. The question of how and why the United Nations is the crux of the great conspiracy to destroy the sovereignty of the United States and the enslavement of the American people within a U.N. one-world dictatorship is a complete and unknown mystery to the vast majority of the American people.

The reason for this unawareness of the frightening danger to our country and to the entire free world is simple. The masterminds behind this great conspiracy have absolute control of all of our mass communications media, especially television, the radio, the press, and Hollywood.

We all know that our State Department, the Pentagon, and the White House have brazenly proclaimed that they have the right and the power to manage the news, to tell us not the truth but what they want us to believe.

They have seized that power on orders from their masters of the great conspiracy and the objective is to brainwash the people into accepting the phony peace bait to transform the United States into an enslaved unit of the United Nations' one-world government.

First of all, bear in mind that the so-called U.N. police action in Korea, was fought by the United States in which 150,000 of our sons were murdered and maimed, was part of the plot; just as the undeclared by Congress war in Vietnam in which our sons died was part of the plot; just as the plot against Rhodesia and South Africa where thousands died was part of the U.N. plot; just as both Gulf Wars, where many thousands of American and allied soldiers died, not to mention the thousands of Iraqi men, women and children we bombed into non-existence.

However, the vitally important thing for all Americans, all you mothers of the boys who died in these wars, to know is that our so-called leaders in Washington, who we elected to safeguard our nation and our constitution, are the betrayers and that behind them are a comparatively small group of men whose sole objective is to enslave the whole world of humanity in their satanic plot of one-world government.

Now in order to give you a very clear picture of this satanic plot, I will go back to its beginning, clear back in the middle of the 18th century and name the men who put that plot into action and then bring you down to the present - today's status of that plot. Now as a matter of further intelligence, a term used by the FBI, let me clarify the meaning of the expression "he is a liberal."

The enemy, meaning the one-world conspirators, have seized upon that word "liberal" as a cover-up for their activities. It sounds so innocent and so humanitarian to be liberal. Well, make sure that the person who calls himself a liberal or is described as a liberal is not in truth a "red."

Now then, this satanic plot was launched back in the 1760's when it first came into existence under the name "Illuminati." This Illuminati was organized by one Adam Weishaupt, born a Jew, who was converted to Catholicism and became a Catholic priest, and then, at the behest of the then newly organized House of Rothschild, defected and organized the Illuminati.

Naturally, the Rothschilds financed that operation and every war since then, beginning with the French Revolution, has been promoted by the Illuminati operating under various names and guises. I say under various names and guises because after the Illuminati was exposed and became notorious, Weishaupt and his co-conspirators began to operate under various other names. In the United States, immediately after World War I, they set up what they called the "Council on Foreign Relations," commonly referred to as the CFR, and this CFR is actually the Illuminati in the United States and its hierarchy.

The masterminds in control of the original Illuminati conspirators are related to those in control of the CFR, but to conceal that fact, most of them changed their original family names to American sounding names. For example, the true name of the

Dillons, Clarence and Douglas Dillon (one Secretary of the U.S. Treasury Department), is Laposky. I'll come back to all this later.

There is a similar establishment of the Illuminati in England operating under the name of the "British Institute of International Affairs." There are similar secret Illuminati organizations in France, Germany, and other nations operating under different names and all these organizations, including the CFR, continuously set up numerous subsidiary or front organizations that are infiltrated into every phase of the various nations' affairs. But at all times, the operations of these organizations were and are masterminded and controlled by the Internationalist Bankers, they in turn were and are controlled by the Rothschilds.

One branch of the Rothschild family had financed Napoleon; another branch of the Rothschilds financed Britain, Germany, and the other nations in the Napoleonic wars.

Immediately after the Napoleonic wars, the Illuminati assumed that all the nations were so destitute and so weary of wars that they'd be glad for any solution, so the Rothschild stooges set up what they called the Congress of Vienna and at that meeting they tried to create the first League of Nations, their first attempted one-world government, on the theory that all the crowned heads of European governments were so deeply in debt to them that they would willingly or unwillingly serve as their stooges.

But the Czar of Russia caught the stench of the plot and completely torpedoed it. The enraged Nathan Rothschild, then the head of the dynasty, vowed that some day he or his descendants would destroy the Czar and his entire family, and his descendants did accomplish that very threat in 1917.

At this point, bear in mind that the Illuminati was not set up to operate on a short-range basis. Normally a conspirator of any type enters into a conspiracy with the expectation of achieving his objective during his own lifetime. But that was not the case with the Illuminati. True, they hoped to accomplish their objective during their lifetime, but paraphrasing "The show must go on," the Illuminati operates on the very long-range basis. Whether it will take scores of years or even centuries, they have dedicated their descendants to keep the pot boiling until they hope the conspiracy is achieved.

Now, let's go back to the birth of the Illuminati. Adam Weishaupt was a Jesuit-trained professor of canon law, teaching in Engelstock University, when he defected from Christianity to embrace the Luciferian conspiracy. It was in 1770 that the professional money lenders, the then recently organized House of Rothschild, retained him to revise and modernize the age-old Protocols of Zionism, which from the outset, was designed to give the Synagogue of Satan, so named by Jesus Christ, ultimate world domination so they could impose the Luciferian ideology upon what would remain of the human race after the final social cataclysm by use of satanic despotism.

Weishaupt completed his task May 1, 1776. Now you know why May 1 is the great day with all communist nations to this very day (May 1 is also "Law Day" as declared by the American Bar Association). That was the day, May 1, 1776, that Weishaupt completed his plan and officially organized the Illuminati to put the plan into execution. That plan required the destruction of all existing governments and religions. That objective was to be reached by dividing the masses of people, whom he Weishaupt, termed: "goyism" or human cattle into opposing camps in ever increasing numbers on political, social, economic, and other issues - the very conditions we have in our country today.

The opposing sides were then to be armed and incidents provided which would cause them to fight and weaken themselves and gradually destroy national governments and religious institutions. Again I say, the very conditions in the world today.

And at this point let me stress a prime feature of the Illuminati plans. When and if their blueprint for world control, the Protocols Of The Elders Of Zion, is discovered and exposed, they would wipe all the Jews off the face of the earth in order to divert suspicions from themselves. If you think this is far fetched, bear in mind that they permitted Hitler, a liberal socialist himself, who was financed by corrupt Kennedy, the Warburgs, and the Rothschilds, to incinerate 6 million Jews.

Now just why did the conspirators choose the word: "Illuminati" for their satanic organization? Weishaupt himself said that the word is derived from Lucifer and means: "holder of the light." He used the lie that his objective was to bring about a one-world government to enable those with mental ability to govern the world and prevent all wars in the future.

In short, using the words: "peace on earth" as his bait, exactly as that same bait as: "peace" was used by the 1945 conspirators to force the United Nations on us, Weishaupt financed, I repeat, by the Rothschilds, recruited some 2,000 paid followers. These included the most intelligent men in the field of arts and letters, education, the sciences, finance, and industry.

He then established Lodges of the Grand Orient; Masonic Lodges to be their secret headquarters and I again repeat, that in all of this he was acting under orders from the House of Rothschild. The main features of the Weishaupt plan of operation required his Illuminati to do the following things to help them to accomplish their purpose:

Use monetary and sex bribery to obtain control of men already in high places in the various levels of all governments and other fields of endeavor. Once influential persons had fallen for the lies, deceits, and temptations of the Illuminati they were to be held in bondage by application of political and other forms of blackmail, threats of financial ruin, public exposure, and fiscal harm, even death to themselves and loved members of their families. Do you realize how many present top officials in our present government in Washington are controlled in just that way by the CFR? Do you realize how many homosexuals in our State Department, the Pentagon, all federal agencies, even in the White House are controlled that way?

Illuminati and the faculties of colleges and universities were to cultivate students possessing exceptional mental ability belonging to well-bred families with international leanings and recommend them for special training in internationalism. Such training was to be provided by granting scholarships to those selected by the Illuminatists. That gives you an idea what a "Rhodes scholarship" means. It means indoctrination into accepting the idea that only a one-world government can put an end to recurring wars and strife. That's how the United Nations was sold to the American people. One of the most notable Rhodes scholars we had in our country was Senator William J. Fulbright, sometimes referred to as half-bright. His entire voting record spells Illuminati. Bill Clinton was another Rhodes scholar. All such scholars were to be first persuaded and then convinced that men of special talent and brains have the right to rule those less gifted on the ground that the masses don't know what is best for them fiscally, mentally, and spiritually.

In addition to the Rhodes and similar scholarships, today there are three special Illuminati schools located in Gordonstown in Scotland, Salem in Germany, and Annavrighta in Greece. These three are known ones, but there are others that are kept undercover. Prince Philip, the husband of Britain's Queen Elizabeth, was educated at Gordonstown at the instigation of Lord Louis Mountbatten, his uncle, a Rothschild relative, who became Britain's Admiral of the Fleet after World War II ended.

All influential people trapped into coming under the control of the Illuminati, plus the students who had been specially educated and trained, were to be used as agents and placed behind the scenes of all governments as experts and specialists so they would advise the top executives to adopt policies which would in the long run serve the secret plans of the Illuminati one-world conspiracy and bring about the destruction of the governments and religions they were elected or appointed to serve.

Do you know how many such men operated in our government at that time? Dean Rusk, Robert McNamara, Hubert Humphrey, Fulbright, Keekle, and goes on and on and on. Today every top level executive of the government is controlled by the Illuminati, including the president.

Perhaps the most vital directive in Weishaupt's plan was to obtain absolute control of the press, at that time the only mass communications media, to distribute information to the public so that all news and information could be slanted so that the masses could be convinced that a one-world government is the only solution to our many and varied problems.

Do you know who owns and controls our mass communications media? I'll tell you. Practically all the movie lots in Hollywood are owned by the Lehmans; Kuhn, Loeb, and Company; Goldman-Sachs; and other internationalist bankers. All the national radio and TV channels in the nation are owned and controlled by those same internationalists bankers.

The same is true of every chain of metropolitan newspapers and magazines, also of the press wire services, such as Associated Press, United Press

International, etc. The supposed heads of all those media are merely the fronts for the internationalist bankers, who in turn compose the hierarchy of the CFR, today's Illuminati in America.

Now can you understand why the Pentagon Press agents, so brazenly proclaimed that the government has the right to lie to the people. What they really mean is that our CFR controlled government had the power to lie to and be believed by the brain-washed American people.

Let us again go back to the first days of the Illuminati. Because Britain and France were the two greatest world powers in the late years of the 18th Century; Weishaupt ordered the Illuminati to foment the colonial wars, including our Revolutionary War, to weaken the British Empire and organize the French Revolution to start in 1789.

However; in 1784, a true act of God placed the Bavarian government in possession of evidence which proved the existence of the Illuminati and that evidence could have saved France if they, the French government, hadn't refused to believe it.

Here is how that act of God happened. It was in 1784 that Weishaupt issued his orders for the French Revolution. A German writer, named Zweig, put it into book form. It contained the entire Illuminati story and Weishaupt's plans. A copy of this book was sent to the Illuminists in France headed by Robespierre whom Weishaupt had delegated to foment the French Revolution.

The courier was struck and killed by lightening as he rode through Rawleston on his way from Frankfurt to Paris. The police found the subversive documents on his body and turned them over to the proper authorities. After a careful study of the plot; the Bavarian government ordered the police to raid Weishaupt's newly organized Lodges of the "Grand Orient" and the homes of his most influential associates.

All additional evidence thus discovered convinced the authorities that the documents were genuine copies of the conspiracy by which the Illuminati planned to use wars and revolutions to bring about the establishment of a one-world government; the powers of which they, headed by the Rothschilds, intended to usurp as soon as it was established, exactly in line with the United Nations' plot of today.

In 1785, the Bavarian government outlawed the Illuminati and closed the

Lodges of the "Grand Orient." In 1786; they published all the details of the conspiracy. The English title of that publication is: "The Original Writings of the Order and the Sect of the Illuminati." Copies of the entire conspiracy were sent to all the heads of church and state in Europe. But the power of the Illuminati, which was actually the power of the Rothschilds, was so great that this warning was ignored. Nevertheless; the Illuminati became a dirty word and it went underground.

At the same time, Weishaupt ordered Illuminists to infiltrate into the Lodges of "Blue Masonry" and formed their own secret societies within all secret societies. Only Masons who proved themselves internationalists and those whose conduct proved they had defected from God were initiated into the Illuminati. Thenceforth; the conspirators donned the cloak of philanthropy and humanitarianism to conceal their revolutionary and subversive activities.

In order to infiltrate into Masonic Lodges in Britain; Weishaupt invited John Robison over to Europe. Robison was a high degree Mason in the "Scottish Rite." He was a professor of natural philosophy at

Edinburgh University and Secretary of the Royal Society of Edinburgh. Robison did not fall for the lie that the objective of the Illuminati was to create a benevolent dictatorship; but he kept his reactions to himself so well that he was entrusted with a copy of Weishaupt's revised conspiracy for study and safekeeping.

Anyway; because the heads of state and church in France were deluded into ignoring the warnings given them; the revolution broke out in 1789 as scheduled by Weishaupt. In order to alert other governments to their danger, in 1798, Robison published a book entitled: "Proof of a Conspiracy to Destroy all Governments and Religions" but his warnings were ignored exactly as our American people have been ignoring all warnings about the United Nations and the Council on Foreign Relations (CFR).

Now here is something that will stun and very likely outrage many who read this; but there is documentary proof that our own Thomas Jefferson and Alexander Hamilton became students of Weishaupt. Jefferson was one of Weishaupt's strongest defenders when he was outlawed by his government and it was Jefferson who infiltrated the

Illuminati into the then newly organized lodges of the "Scottish Rite" in New England. Here is the proof.

In 1789; John Robison warned all Masonic leaders in America that the Illuminati had infiltrated into their lodges and on July 19, 1789; David Papen, President of Harvard University, issued the same warning to the graduating class and lectured them on how the influence of Illuminism was acquitting on American politics and religion, and to top it off; John Quincy Adams, who had organized the New England Masonic Lodges, issued his warnings.

Adams wrote three letters to Colonel William L. Stone, a top Mason, in which he exposed how Jefferson was using Masonic lodges for subversive Illuministic purposes. Those three letters are at this very time in Whittenburg Square Library in Philadelphia. In short; Jefferson, founder of the Democratic Party, was a member of the Illuminati which at least partly accounts for the condition of the party at this time and through infiltration of the Republican Party; we have exactly nothing of loyal Americanism today.

That disastrous rebuff at the Congress

of Vienna created by the Czar of Russia, Alexander I, did not by any means destroy the Illuminati conspiracy. It merely forced them to adopt a new strategy realizing that the one-world idea was, for the moment, killed. The Rothschild's decided that to keep the plot alive they would have to do it by heightening their control of the money system of the European nations.

Earlier, by a ruse the outcome of the Battle of Waterloo had been falsified, Rothschild had spread a story that Napoleon had won the battle which precipitated a terrific panic on the stock market in England. All stocks had plummeted down to practically zero and Nathan Rothschild bought all the stocks for virtually a penny on its dollar values.

That gave him complete control of the economy of Britain and virtually of all Europe. So immediately after that Congress in Vienna had boomeranged; Rothschild had forced Britain to set up a new "Bank of England" which he had absolute control exactly, as later through Jacob Schiff; he engineered our own "Federal Reserve Act" which gave the House of Rothschild a secret control of the economy in the United States. But now for a moment; let's dwell on the activities of the Illuminati in the United States.

In 1826; one Captain William Morgan decided it was his duty to inform all Masons and the general public what the full proof was regarding the Illuminati, their secret plans, intended objectives, and to reveal the identities of the masterminds of the conspiracy. The Illuminati promptly tried Morgan in absentia and convicted him of treason.

They ordered one Richard Howard, an English Illuminist, to carry out their sentence of execution as a traitor. Morgan was warned and he tried to escape to Canada, but Howard caught up with him near the border; near the Niagara Gorge to be exact, where he murdered him. This was verified in a sworn statement made in New York by one Avery Allen to the effect that he heard Howard render his report of the execution to a meeting of "Knights Templers" in St. John's Hall in New York. He also told how arrangements had been made to ship Howard back to England.

That Allen affidavit is on record in New York City Archives. Very few Masons and very few of the general public know that general disapproval over that incident of murder caused approximately half of all the Masons in the northern jurisdiction of the United States to secede. Copies of the minutes of the meeting held to discuss that matter are still in existence in safe hands and that all that secrecy emphasizes the power of the masterminds of the Illuminati to prevent such terrible events of history from being taught in our schools.

In the early 1850's; the Illuminati held a secret meeting in New York which was addressed by a British Illuminist named Wright. Those in attendance were told that the Illuminati was organizing to unite the Nihilist and Atheist groups with all other subversive groups into an international group to be known as Communists. That was when the word: "communist" first came into being and it was intended to be the supreme weapon and scare word to terrify the whole world and drive the terrorized peoples into the Illuminati one-world scheme.

This scheme: "communism," was to be used to enable the Illuminati to foment future wars and revolutions. Clinton Roosevelt, a direct ancestor of Franklin Roosevelt; Horace Greeley; and Charles Dana; foremost newspaper publishers of that time were appointed to head a committee to raise funds for the new venture. Of course, most of the funds were provided by the Rothschilds and this fund was used to finance Karl Marx and Engels when they wrote "Das Kaptial" and the "Communist Manifesto" in Soho, England. And this clearly reveals that communism is not a so-called ideology, but a secret weapon; a bogy man word to serve the purpose of the Illuminati.

Weishaupt died in 1830; but prior to his death, he prepared a revised version of the age-old conspiracy, the Illuminati, which under various aliases was to organize, finance, direct, and control all international organizations and groups by working their agents into executive positions at the top.

In the United States we have Woodrow Wilson, Franklin Roosevelt, Jack Kennedy, Lyndon Johnson, Dean Rusk, Robert McNamara, William Fulbright, Bill and Hillary Clinton, George Bush Sr. and George Bush, Jr. and Barak Obama as prime examples.

In addition, while Karl Marx was writing the "Communist Manifesto" under the director of one group of Illuminists, Professor Karl Ritter of Frankfurt University was writing the antithesis under the direction of another group.

The idea was that those who direct the overall conspiracy could use the differences in those two so-called ideologies to enable them to divide larger and larger members of the human race into opposing camps so that they could be armed and then brainwashed into fighting and destroying each other, and particularly, to destroy all political and religious institutions.

The work Ritter started was continued after his death and completed by the German philosopher Freidrich Wilhelm Nietzache who founded Nietzscheanism. This Nietzecheanism was later developed into Fascism and then into Nazism and was used to foment World War I and II.

In 1834 the Italian revolutionary leader, Guiseppe Mazzini, was selected by the Illuminati to direct their revolutionary program throughout the world. He served in that capacity until he died in 1872, but some years before he died, Mazzini had enticed an American General named Albert Pike into the Illuminati. Pike was fascinated by the idea of a one-world government and ultimately he became the head of this Luciferian conspiracy.

Between 1859 and 1871 he, Pike,

worked out a military blueprint for three world wars and various revolutions throughout the world which he considered would forward the conspiracy to its final stage in the 20th century. Again I remind you that these conspirators were never concerned with immediate success. They also operated on a long-range view.

Pike did most of his work in his home in Little Rock, Arkansas. But a few years later; when the Illuminati's Lodges of the Grand Orient became suspect and repudiated because of Mazzini's revolutionary activities in Europe, Pike organized what he called the New and Reformed Palladian Right.

He set up three Supreme Councils; one in Charleston, South Carolina, one in Rome, Italy, and a third in Berlin, Germany. He had Mazzini establish 23 subordinate councils in strategic locations throughout the world. These have been the secret headquarters of the world revolutionary movement ever since.

Long before Marconi invented the radio, the scientists in the Illuminati had found the means for Pike and the heads of his councils to communicate secretly. It was the discovery of that secret that enabled intelligence officers to understand how apparently unrelated incidents, such as the assassination of an Austrian Prince, Arch Duke Ferdinand I, at Serbia, took place simultaneously throughout the world which developed into a war or a revolution.

Pike's plan was as simple as it has proved effective. It called for Communism, Nazism, political Zionism, and other international movements to be organized and used to foment three global world wars and at least two major revolutions.

The First World War was to be fought so as to enable the Illuminati to destroy Czarism in Russia, as vowed by Rothschild after the Czar had torpedoed his scheme at the Congress in Vienna, and to transform Russia into a stronghold of atheistic communism. The differences stirred up by agents of the Illuminati between the British and German Empires were to be used to foment this war. After the war would be ended, communism was to be built up and used to destroy other governments and weaken religions.

World War II, when and if necessary, was to be fomented by using the controversies between Fascists and political Zionists, and here let it be noted that Hitler was financed by Krupp, the Warburgs, the Rothschilds, and other internationalist bankers and that the slaughter of the 6 million Jews by Hitler didn't bother the Jewish internationalist bankers at all.

That slaughter was necessary in order to create worldwide hatred of the German people and thus bring about war against them. In short; this Second World War was to be fought to destroy Nazism and increase the power of political Zionism so that the state of Israel could be established in Palestine.

During this World War II, international communism was to be built up until it equaled in strength to that of the united Christendom. When it reached that point, it was to be contained and kept in check until required for the final social cataclysm. As we know now, Roosevelt, Churchill, and Stalin put that exact policy into effect and Truman, Eisenhower, Kennedy, Johnson, both George Bushes. Clinton and Obama continued that same exact policy.

World War III is to be fomented by using the so-called controversies, the agents of the Illuminati operating under whatever new name, as are now being stored up between the political Zionists and the leaders of the Moslem world. That war is to be directed in such a manner that all of Islam and political Zionism (Israel) will destroy each other while at the same time; the remaining nations once more divided on this issue will be forced to fight themselves into a state of complete exhaustion, physically, mentally, spiritually, and economically.

Now, can any thinking person doubt that the intrigue now going on in the near Middle and Far East is designed to accomplish that satanic objective? Albert Pike himself foretold all this in a statement he made to Mazzini on August 15, 1871. Pike stated that after World War III is ended, those who will aspire to undisputed world domination will provoke the greatest social cataclysm the world has ever known. Quoting his own words taken from the letter he wrote to Mazzini and which letter is now catalogued in the British Museum in London, England; he said:

"We shall unleash the nihilists and the atheists and we shall provoke a great social cataclysm which in all its horror will show clearly to all nations the effect of absolute atheism, the origins of savagery and of most bloody turmoil. Then everywhere, the people will be forced to defend themselves against the world minority of the world revolutionaries and will exterminate those destroyers of civilization and the multitudes disillusioned with Christianity whose spirits will be from that moment without direction and leadership and anxious for an ideal, but without knowledge where to send its adoration, will receive the true light through the universal manifestation of the pure doctrine of Lucifer brought finally out into public view. A manifestation which will result from a general reactionary movement which will follow the destruction of Christianity and Atheism both conquered and exterminated at the same time."

CHAPTER TWO

When Mazzini died in 1872; Pike made another revolutionary leader named Adrian Lemmy his successor. Lemmy, in turn, was succeeded by Lenin and Trotsky, then by Stalin. The revolutionary activities of all those men were financed by British, French, German, and American international bankers - all of them dominated by the House of Rothschilds.

We are supposed to believe that the international bankers of today, like the money changers of Christ's day, are only the tools or agents of the great conspiracy, but actually they are the masterminds behind all the mass communications media leading us into believing that communism is a movement of the so-called workers; the actual fact is that both British and American intelligence officers have authentic documentary evidence that international liberals, operating through their international banking houses, particularly the House of Rothschilds, have financed both sides of every war and revolution since 1776.

Those who today comprise the conspiracy (the CFR in the United States) direct our governments whom they hold in usury through such methods as the Federal Reserve System in America to fight wars, such as Vietnam (created by the United Nations), so as to further Pike's Illuminati plans to bring the world to that stage of the conspiracy when atheistic communism and the whole of Christianity can be forced into an all out third world war within each remaining nation as well as on an international basis scale.

The headquarters of the great conspiracy in the late 1700's was in Frankfurt, Germany where the House of Rothschild had been established by Mayar (or Mayer) Amschel who adopted the Rothschild name and linked together other international financiers who had literally sold their souls to the devil. After the Bavarian government's exposure in 1786, the conspirators moved their headquarters to Switzerland then to London. Since World War II (after Jacob Schiff, the Rothschild's boy in America died), the headquarters of the American branch has been in the Harold Pratt Building in New York City and the Rockefellers, originally proteges of Schiff, have taken over the manipulation of finances in America for the Illuminati.

In the final phases of the conspiracy, the one-world government will consist of the king-dictator, the head of the United Nations, the CFR, and a few billionaires, economists, and scientists who have proved their devotion to the great conspiracy. All others are to be integrated into a vast conglomeration of mongrolized humanity, actually slaves.

Now let me show you how our federal government and the American people have been sucked into the one-world take over plot of the Illuminati great conspiracy and always bear in mind, that the United Nations was created to become the housing for that one-world, liberal conspiracy. The real foundations of the plot of the takeover of the United States were laid during the period of our Civil War. Not that Weishaupt and the earlier masterminds had ever overlooked the new world, as I have previously indicated, Weishaupt had his agents planted over here as far back as the

Revolutionary War, but George Washington was more than a match for them.

It was during the Civil War that the conspirators launched their first concrete efforts. We know that Judah Benjamin, chief advisor of Jefferson Davis, was a Rothschild agent. We also know that there were Rothschild agents planted in Abraham Lincoln's cabinet who tried to sell him into a financial dealing with the House of Rothschild.

But old Abe saw through the scheme and bluntly rejected it thereby incurring the undying enmity of the Rothschilds, exactly as the Russian Czar did when he torpedoed their first League of Nations at the Congress in Vienna. Investigation of the assassination of Lincoln revealed that the assassin John Wilkes Booth was a member of a secret conspiratorial group. Because there was a number of highly important government officials involved, the name of the group was never revealed and it became a mystery exactly as the assassination of Jack Kennedy is still a mystery. But I am sure it will not remain a mystery for long.

Anyway, the ending of the Civil War destroyed temporarily all chances of the House of Rothschilds to get a clutch on our money system such as they had acquired in Britain and other nations in Europe. I say temporarily because the Rothschilds and the masterminds of the conspiracy never quit so they had to start from scratch, but they lost no time in getting started.

Jacob H. Schiff

Shortly after the Civil War; a young immigrant, who called himself Jacob H. Schiff, arrived in New York. Jacob was a young man with a mission for the House of Rothschild. Jacob was the son of a Rabbi who was born in one of the Rothschild's houses in Frankfurt, Germany.

I will not go deeply into his background. The important point was that Rothschild recognized in him not only a potential money wizard, but more important, he also saw the latent Machiavellian qualities in Jacob that could, as it did, make him an invaluable functionary in the great one-world conspiracy.

After a comparatively brief training period in the Rothschild's London Bank, Jacob left for America with instructions to buy into a banking house which was to be the springboard to acquire control of the money system of the United States. Actually, Jacob came here to carry out four specific assignments.

1. The most important was to acquire control of America's money system.

2. Find desirable men, who for a price, would be willing to serve as stooges for the great conspiracy and promote them into high places in our federal government, our Congress, and the U.S. Supreme Court, and all Federal agencies.

3. Create minority group strife throughout the nations, particularly between the whites and blacks.

4. Create a movement to destroy religion in the United States, but Christianity to be the chief target.

Earlier I stated that Jacob Schiff came to America with orders by Rothschild to carry out four specific directives. The first and most important one was to get control of the United States' money system. Let's trace Schiff's steps to accomplish that directive. As a first step he had to buy into a banking house, but it had to be the kind of a house that he could absolutely control and mold for that primary objective of entrapping our U.S. money system.

After carefully scouting around, Jacob bought a partnership in a firm that called itself: Kuhn and Loeb. Like Schiff, Kuhn and Loeb were immigrants from German Jewish ghettos. They came to the U.S. in the mid 1840's and both of them started their business careers as itinerant pack peddlers. In the early 1850's, they pooled their interests and set up a merchandise store in Lafayette, Indiana under the firm name of Kuhn and Loeb servicing the covered wagon settlers on their way west. In the years that followed, they set up similar stores in Cincinnati and St. Louis. Then they added pawn broking to their merchandising pursuits. From that to money lending was a short and quick step.

By the time Schiff arrived on the scene, Kuhn and Loeb was a well-known private banking firm and this is the firm Jacob bought into. Shortly after he became a partner in Kuhn and Loeb; Schiff married Loeb's daughter, Teresa, then he bought out Kuhn's interests and moved the firm to New York and Kuhn and Loeb became Kuhn, Loeb, and Company, international bankers with Jacob Schiff, agent of the Rothschilds, ostensibly the sole owner. And throughout his career, this blend of Judas and Machiavelli, the first heirarch of the Illuminati's great conspiracy in America, posed as a generous philanthropist and a man of great holiness, the cover-up policy set forth by the Illuminati.

As I have stated, the first great step of the conspiracy was to be the entrapment of our money system. To achieve that objective, Schiff had to get full cooperation of the then big banker elements in America, and that was easier said than done. Even in those years, Wall Street was the heart of the American money mart and J.P. Morgan was its dictator. Next in line were the Drexels and the Biddles of Philadelphia. All the other financiers, big and little, danced to the music of those three houses, but particularly to that of Morgan. All of those three were proud, haughty, arrogant potentates.

For the first few years, they viewed the little bewhiskered man from the German ghettos with utter contempt, but Jacob knew how to overcome that. He threw a few Rothschild bones to them - said bones being distribution in America of desirable European stock and bond issues. Then he discovered that he had a still more potent weapon in his hands in the following.

It was in the decades following our Civil War that our industries began to burgeon. We had great railroads to build. The oil, mining, steel, textile industries were bursting out of their swaddling clothes. All of that called for vast financing, much of that financing had to come from abroad. That meant the House of Rothschild and that was when Schiff came into his own. He played a very crafty game.

He became the patron saint of John D. Rockefeller, Edward R. Harriman, and Andrew Carnegie. He financed the Standard Oil Company for Rockefeller, the Railroad Empire for Harriman, and the Steel Empire for Carnegie. But instead of hogging all the other industries for Kuhn, Loeb, and Company, he opened the doors of the House of Rothschild to Morgan, Biddle, and Drexel. In turn, Rothschild arranged the setting up of London, Paris, European and other branches for those three, but always in partnerships with Rothschild subordinates and Rothschild made it very clear to all those men that Schiff was to be the boss in New York.

Thus at the turn of the century Schiff had a tight control of the entire banking fraternity on Wall Street which by then, with Schiff's help, included Lehman brothers, Goldman-Sachs, and other internationalist banks that where headed by men chosen by the Rothschilds. In short, that meant control of the nation's money powers and he was then ready for the giant step - the entrapment of our national money system.

Now under our Constitution, all control of our money system is vested solely in our Congress. Schiff's next important step was to seduce our Congress to betray that Constitutional edict by surrendering that control to the hierarchy of the Illuminati's great conspiracy. In order to legalize that surrender and thus make the people powerless to resist it, it would be necessary to have Congress enact special legislation.

To accomplish that, Schiff would have to infiltrate stooges into both houses of Congress - stooges powerful enough to railroad Congress into passing such legislation. Equally or even more important, he would have to plant a stooge in the White House, a president that is without integrity and without scruples who would sign that legislation into law. To accomplish that, he had to get control of either the Republican or the Democratic Party.

The Democratic Party was the more vulnerable; it was the hungrier of the two parties. Except for Grover Cleveland, the Democrats had been unable to land one of their men in the White House since before the Civil War. There were two reasons for that:

1. Poverty of the Party.

There were considerably more Republican-minded voters than Democrats. The poverty matter was not a great problem, but the voter problem was a different story.

But as I previously said, Schiff was a smart cookie.

Here is the atrocious and murderous method he employed to solve that voter problem. His solution emphasizes how very little the Jewish internationalist bankers care about their own racial brethren as you shall see.

Suddenly, around 1890, there broke out a nationwide series of pogroms in Russia. Many, many, thousands of innocent Jews, men, women, and children were slaughtered by the Cossacks and other peasants. Similar pogroms with similar slaughter of innocent Jews broke out in Poland, Rumania, and Bulgaria. All those pogroms were fomented by Rothschild agents. As a result, the Jewish terrified refugees from all of those nations swarmed into the United States and that continued throughout the next two or three decades because the pogroms were continuous through all those years. All those refugees were aided by self-styled humanitarian committees set up by Schiff, the Rothschilds, and all the Rothschild affiliates.

In the main; the refugees streamed into New York, but the Schiff-Rothschild humanitarian committees found ways to shuffle many of them into other large cities such as Chicago, Boston, Philadelphia, Detroit, and Los Angeles. All of them were quickly transformed into "naturalized citizens" and educated to register as Democrats. Thus all of that minority group became solid Democratic voter blocks in their communities all controlled and maneuvered by their so-called benefactors. And shortly after the turn of the century, they became vital factors in the political life of our nation. That was one of the methods Schiff employed to plant men like Nelson Aldrich in our Senate and Woodrow Wilson in the White House.

2. Racial Strife.

At this point let me remind you of another one of the important jobs that was assigned to Schiff when he was dispatched to America. I refer to the job of destroying the unity of the American people by creating minority group and racial strife. By the pogrom-driven Jewish refugees into America, Schiff was creating a ready-made minority group for that purpose. But the

Jewish people, as a whole, made fearful by the pogroms, could not be depended upon to create the violence necessary to destroy the unity of American people.

But right within America, there was an already made-to-order, although as yet, a sleeping minority group, the Negroes, who could be sparked into demonstrations, rioting, looting, murder, and every other type of lawlessness - all that was necessary was to incite and arouse them. Together, those two minority groups, properly maneuvered, could be used to create exactly the King of Strife in America the Illuminati would need to accomplish their objective.

Thus at the same time that Schiff and co-conspirators were laying their plans for the entrapment of our money system, they were also perfecting plans to hit the unsuspecting American people with an explosive and terrifying racial upheaval that would tear the people into hate fractions and create chaos throughout the nation, especially on all college and university campuses; all protected by Earl Warren decisions and our so-called leaders in Washington D.C. (Remember the Warren commission on the assassination of

President John F. Kennedy). Of course, perfecting those plans require time and infinitely patient organizing.

Jack Kennedy, during his term of office as the President of the United States, became a Christian. In his attempt to repent, he tried to inform the people of this Nation (at least twice) that the Office of the President of the United States was being manipulated by the Illuminati/CFR.

At the same time, he put a stop to the 'borrowing' of Federal Reserve Notes from the Federal Reserve Bank and began issuing United States Notes (which was interest free) on the credit of the United States. It was the issuing of the United States Notes that caused Jack Kennedy to be assassinated.

Upon taking the Oath of Office, Lyndon B. Johnson stopped the issuing of the United States Notes and went back to borrowing Federal Reserve Bank Notes (which was loaned to the people of the United States at the going rate of interest of 17%). The US Notes that was issued under John F. Kennedy, was of the 1963 series which had a "Red" seal on the face of the Note.

Now to remove all doubts, I'll take a few moments to give you the documentary proof of this racial strife plot. First of all they had to create the leadership and organizations to draw in millions of dupes, both Jewish and Negroes, who would do the demonstrating and commit the rioting, looting, and lawlessness.

So in 1909, Schiff, the Lehmans, and other conspirators, organized and set up the National Association for the Advancement of the Colored People known as the "NAACP." The presidents, directors, and legal councils of the NAACP were always "white men Jews" appointed by Schiff.

Then in 1913, the Schiff group organized the Anti-defamation League of the B'nai B'rith commonly known as the "ADL" to serve as the Gestapo and hatchet man outfit for the entire great conspiracy. Today the sinister ADL maintains over 2,000 agencies in all parts of our country and they advise and completely control every action of the NAACP or of the Urban League of all the other Negro civil rights organizations throughout the nation including such leaders as Martin Luther King, Stockely Carmichael, Barnard Rustin, and others of the ilk.

CHAPTER THREE

By 1917 the conspirators had achieved their primary objective; all of Europe was in a state of destitution. All the peoples were war weary and crying for peace and the outcome too was all set. It was to come as soon as the United States would be hurled on the side of the Allies and that was all set to happen immediately after Wilson's re-election. After that, there could be only one outcome; complete victory for the Allies. To fully confirm my statement that long before 1917, the conspiracy, headed in America by Jacob Schiff, had it all set to hurl the United States into that war. I will cite the proof:

When Wilson was campaigning for re-election in 1916, his chief appeal was: "re-elect the man who will keep your sons out of the war." But during that same campaign, the Republican Party publicly charged that Wilson had long committed himself to throw us into the war. They charged that if he would be defeated he would accomplish that act during his few remaining months in office, but if re-elected, he would hold off until after the election. But at that time the American people looked upon Wilson as a "God-man." Well, Wilson was re-elected and as per the schedule of the conspirators he hurled us into the war in 1917. He used the sinking of the Lusitania as an excuse - a sinking which also was prearranged. Roosevelt, also a God-man in the eyes of the American people, followed the same technique in 1941 when he used the prearranged Pearl Harbor attack as his excuse for hurling us into World War II.

Now exactly as the conspirators planned, victory for the Allies would eliminate all the Monarchs of the defeated Nations and leave all their people leaderless, confused, bewildered and perfectly conditioned for the one-world government. The great conspiracy intended would follow, but there still would be an obstacle; the same obstacle that had balked the Illuminati and Rothschild at that Congress in Vienna (peace gathering) after the Napoleonic Wars.

Russia would be on the winning side this time as it was in 1814 and therefore the Czar would be securely seated on his throne. Here it is pertinent to note that Russia, under the Czarist regime, had been the one country in which the Illuminati had never made any headway nor had the Rothschilds ever been able to infiltrate in their banking interests thus a winning Czar would be more difficult than ever to cope with. Even if he could be enticed into a "League of Nations" it was a foregone conclusion that he would never go for a one-world government.

So even before the outbreak of World War I, the conspirators had a plan in the making to carry out Nathan Rothschild's vow of 1814 to destroy the Czar and also murder all possible royal heirs to the throne and it would have to be done before the close of the war. The Russian Bolsheviks were to be their instruments in this particular plot. From the turn of the century, the chiefs of the Bolsheviks were Nicolai Lenin, Leon Trotsky, and later Joseph Stalin.

Of course, those were not their true family names. Prior to the outbreak Switzerland became their haven. Trotsky's headquarters was on the lower East Side in

New York, largely the habitat of Russian-Jewish refugees. Both Lenin and Trotsky were similarly bewhiskered and unkempt. In those days that was the badge of Bolshevism. Both lived well yet neither had a regular occupation.

Neither had any visible means of support, yet both always had plenty of money. All those mysteries were solved in 1917. Right from the outset of the war strange and mysterious goings on were taking place in New York. Night after night, Trotsky darted furtively in and out of Jacob Schiff's palace mansion and in the dead of those same nights there were a gathering of hoodlums of New York's lower East Side. All of them Russian refugees at Trotsky's headquarters and all were going through some mysterious sort of training process that was all shrouded in mystery. Nobody talked, although it did leak out that Schiff was financing all of Trotsky's activities.

Then suddenly Trotsky vanished and so did approximately 300 of his trained hoodlums. Actually they were on the high seas in a Schiff-chartered ship bound for a rendezvous with Lenin and his gang in Switzerland. And also on that ship was

$20,000,000 in gold; the $20,000,000 was provided to finance the Bolsheviks takeover of Russia. In anticipation of Trotsky's arrival, Lenin prepared to throw a party in his Switzerland hideaway.

Men of the very highest places in the world were to be guests at that party. Among them were the mysterious Colonel Edward Mandell House, Woodrow Wilson's mentor and more important, Schiff's special and confidential messenger. Another of the expected guests was Warburg of the Warburg Banking Clan in Germany who was financing the Kaiser and whom the Kaiser had rewarded by making him chief of the Secret Police of Germany. In addition, there were the Rothschilds of London and Paris also Lithenoth, Kakonavich, and Stalin (who was then the head of a train and bank robbing gang of bandits). He was known as the "Jesse James of the Urals."

And here I must remind you that England and France were then long in the war with Germany and that on February 3, 1917, Wilson had broken off all diplomatic relations with Germany. Therefore, Warburg, Colonel House, the Rothschilds, and all those others were enemies, but of course, Switzerland was neutral ground where enemies could meet and be friends, especially if they had some scheme in common.

That Lenin party was very nearly wrecked by an unforeseen incident. The Schiff-chartered ship on its way to Switzerland was intercepted and taken into custody by a British warship. But Schiff quickly rushed orders to Wilson to order the British to release the ship intact with Trotsky's hoodlums and the gold. Wilson obeyed. He warned the British that if they refuse to release the ship; the United States would not enter the war in April as he had faithfully promised a year earlier.

The British headed the warning. Trotsky arrived in Switzerland and the Lenin party went off as scheduled, but they still faced what ordinarily would have been the insurmountable obstacle of getting the Lenin-Trotsky band of terrorists across the border into Russia. Well, that's where Brother Warburg, chief of the German Secret Police came in. He loaded all those thugs into sealed freight cars and made all the necessary arrangements for their secret entry into Russia. The rest is history. The revolution in Russia took place and all members of the royal Romanoff family were murdered.

Now my chief objective is to establish beyond even a remote doubt that communism, so-called, is an integral part of the Illuminati great conspiracy for the enslavement of the entire world. That communism is merely their weapon and bogy man word to terrify the peoples of the whole world and that the conquest of Russia and the creation of communism was, in great part, organized by Schiff and the other international bankers right in our own city of New York.

A fantastic story? Yes. Some might even refuse to believe it. Well, for the benefit of any doubting Thomas I will prove it by reminding that just a few years ago Charlie Knickerbocker, a Hearst newspaper columnist, published an interview with John Schiff, grandson of Jacob, in which young Schiff confirmed the entire story and named the figure Jacob contributed, $20,000,000.

If anybody still has even a remote doubt that the entire menace of communism was created by the masterminds of the great conspiracy right in our own city of New York, I will cite the following historical fact. All records show that when Lenin and Trotsky engineered the capture of Russia, they operated as heads of the Bolsheviks party. Now "Bolshevism" is a purely Russian word.

The masterminds realized that "Bolshevism" could never be sold as an ideology to any but the Russian people. So in April 1918, Jacob Schiff dispatched Colonel House to Moscow with orders to Lenin, Trotsky, and Stalin to change the name of their regime to the Communist Party and to adopt the Karl Marx "Manifesto" as the constitution of the Communist Party. Lenin, Trotsky, and Stalin obeyed, and in that year of 1918 was when the Communist party and the menace of communism came into being. All this is confirmed in Webster's Collegiate Dictionary, Fifth Edition.

In short, communism was created by the capitalists. Thus, until November 11, 1918, the entire fiendish plan of the conspirators worked perfectly. All the great nations, including the United States, were war-weary, devastated, and mourning their dead. Peace was the great universal desire. Thus when it was proposed by Wilson to set up a "League of Nations" to ensure peace, all the great nations, with no Russian Czar to stand in their way, jumped on that bandwagon without even stopping to read the fine print in that insurance policy.

That is, all but one: the United States, the very one that Schiff and his co-conspirators least expected would balk and that was their one fatal mistake in that early plot. You see, when Schiff planted Woodrow Wilson in the White House the conspirators assumed that they had the United States in the proverbial bag. Wilson had been perfectly built up as a great humanitarian. He supposedly became established as a God-man with the American people. There was every reason for the conspirators to have believed that he would easily hornswaggled Congress into buying the "League of Nations," sight unseen, exactly as the Congress of 1945 bought the "United Nations," sight unseen.

But there was one man in the Senate in 1918 who saw through that scheme just as the Russian Czar did in 1814. He was a man of great political stature, almost as great as that of Teddy Roosevelt and fully as astute. He was highly respected and trusted by all members of both houses of Congress and by the American people. The name of that great and patriotic American was Henry Cabot Lodge (not the phony who called himself Henry Cabot Lodge, Jr., until he was exposed).

Henry Cabot Lodge completely unmasked Wilson and kept the United States out of the "League of Nations."

Shortly thereafter, the Illuminati had created the 17th Amendment to do away with appointed Senators by the legislatures of the several states of the Union. Whereas the Illuminati controls the press; they now control the election of the US Senators. The Illuminati/CFR had little or no power over the individual legislatures of the several states or their appointed U.S. Senators prior to the [purported] ratification of the 17th Amendment.

Although the 17th Amendment supposedly amends the method of placing Senators into the US Senate, the 17th Amendment was never ratified in accordance to the last sentence of Article V of the US Constitution. Two states, New

Jersey and Utah, voted down the proposition and nine other states never voted at all.

Whereas the states of New Jersey and Utah expressly refused to relinquish their "suffrage" in the Senate while the other non-voting nine states never gave their "express" consent; the proposition for the 17th Amendment did not obtain the "unanimous" vote required for its adoption. Furthermore, the resolution that created the "Proposition" did not pass the Senate with a "unanimous" vote and as those Senators of that day were "appointed" by the legislatures of their states, those "negative" votes or "non-votes" were made in the name of their respective state.

Here it becomes of great interest to know the real reason for the Wilson League of Nations flop. As I previously stated, Schiff was sent to the United States to carry out four specific assignments:

1. Most important was to acquire complete control of the U.S. money system.

2. As outlined in the original Weishaupt Illuminati blueprint, he was to find the right

kind of men to serve as stooges for the great conspiracy and promote them into the highest offices in our federal government, our Congress, our U.S. Supreme Court, and all federal agencies, such as the State Department, the Pentagon, the Treasury Department, etc.

3. Destroy the unity of the American people by creating minority groups strife throughout the nation, especially between the whites and blacks as outlined in Israel Cohen's book.

4. Create a movement to destroy religion of the United States with Christianity to be the chief target or victim.

In addition, he was strongly reminded of the imperative directive of the Illuminati blueprint to achieve full control of all mass communications media to be used to brainwash the people into believing and accepting all of the maneuverings of the great conspiracy. Schiff was warned that only control of the press, at that time our only mass communications media, would enable him to destroy the unity of the American people.

Now then, Schiff and his co-conspirators did set up the "NAACP" (the "National Association for the Advancement of the Colored People") in 1909 and in 1913 he set up the "Anti defamation League of the B'nai B'rith;" both were to create the necessary strife, but in the early years; the "ADL" operated very timidly. Perhaps for fear of a "pogrom-like" action by an aroused and enraged American people and the "NAACP" was practically dormant because its white leadership didn't realize that they would have to develop fire-brand Negro leaders, such as Martin Luther King for one, to spark the then completely satisfied contented mass of Negroes.

In addition, he, Schiff, was busy developing and infiltrating the stooges to serve in all high places in our Washington government and in the job of acquiring control of our money system and the creation of the "16th Amendment." He also was very busy with the organizing of the plot for the takeover of Russia.

In short, Schiff was kept so busy with all those jobs that he completely overlooked the supreme job of acquiring complete control of our mass communications media. That oversight was a direct cause for Wilson's failure to lure the United States into the "League of Nations" because when Wilson decided to go to the people to overcome the opposition of the Lodge-controlled Senate, despite his established, but phony reputation as a great humanitarian, he found himself faced by a solidly united people and by a loyal press whose only ideology was "Americanism" and the American way of life.

At that time, due to the ineptness and ineffectiveness of the "ADL" and the "NAACP," there were no organized minority groups; no Negro problems; no so-called antisemetic problems to sway the people's thinking. There were no "lefts" and there were no "rights" nor any prejudices for crafty exploitations. Thus Wilson's "League of Nations" appeal fell on deaf ears. That was the end of Woodrow Wilson, the conspirators great humanitarian. He quickly abandoned his crusade and returned to Washington were he shortly died an imbecile brought on by syphilis and that was the end of the

"League of Nations" as a corridor into one-world government.

Of course that debacle was a terrible disappointment to the masterminds of the Illuminati conspiracy, but they were not discouraged. As I have previously stressed, this enemy never quits; they simply decided to reorganize and try from scratch again. By this time Schiff was very old and slow. He knew it. He knew that the conspiracy needed a new younger and more active leadership.

So on his orders, Colonel House and Bernard Barouk organized and set up what they called the "Council on Foreign Relations," the new name under which the Illuminati would continue to function in the United States. The hierarchy, officers, and directors of the CFR is composed principally of descendants of the original Illuminati, many of whom who had abandoned their old family name and acquired new Americanized names.

For one example, we had Douglas Dillon, who was then Secretary of Treasury of the United States, whose original name was Laposky. Another example was Pauley, head of the CBS TV channel, whose true name is Palinsky. The membership of the CFR is approximately 1,000 in number and contains the heads of virtually every industrial empire in America such as Blough, then president of the U.S. Steel Corporation; Rockefeller, king of the oil industry; Henry Ford, II, and so on, and of course all the international bankers.

Also, the heads of the "tax-free" foundations are officers and/or active CFR members. In short, all the men who provided the money and the influence to elect the CFR-chosen Presidents of the United States, the Congressmen, the Senators, and who decide the appointments of our various Secretaries of State, of the Treasury, of every important federal agency are members of the CFR and they are very obedient members indeed.

Now just to cement that fact, I will mention the names of the United States Presidents who were members of the CFR: Franklin Roosevelt, Herbert Hoover, Dwight D. Eisenhower, Jack Kennedy also, Nixon, Clinton and the George Bushes when they later became U.S. President. Others who were considered for the presidency were Thomas E. Dewey, Adlai Stevenson, and vice-president of a CFR subsidiary, Barry Goldwater. Among the important cabinet members of the various administrations we had John Foster Dulles, Allen Dulles, Cordell Hull, John J. MacLeod, Robert Morganthau, Clarence Dillon, Dean Rusk, Robert McNamara, and just to emphasize the "red color" of the "CFR," we have had members of such men as Alger Hess, Ralph Bunche, Pusvolsky, Haley Dexter White (real name Weiss), Owen Lattimore, Phillip Jaffey. Simultaneously, they were flooding thousands of homosexuals and other black malleable characters into all the federal agencies from the White House on down. Do you remember Johnson's great friends Jenkins and Bobby Baker?

Now there were many jobs the new CFR had to accomplish. They required much help. So their first job was to set up various "subsidiaries" to whom they assigned special objectives. I can't name all the subsidiaries in this article, but the following are a few: the "Foreign Policy Association" ("FPA"), the "World Affairs Council" ("WAC"), the "Business Advisory Council" ("BAC"), the notorious "ADA" ("Americans for Democratic Action" virtually headed by Walter Ruther), the notorious "13-13" in Chicago. Barry

Goldwater was a vice-president of one of the CFR subsidiaries. In addition, the CFR set up special committees in every state in the Union to whom they assigned the various state operations.

Simultaneously, the Rothschilds set up similar CFR-like control groups in England, France, Germany, and other Nations to control world conditions and cooperate with the CFR to bring about another world war. But the CFR's first and foremost job was to get complete control of our mass communications media.

The control of the press was assigned to Rockefeller. Thus, Henry Luce was financed to set up a number of national magazines, among them "Life," "Time," "Fortune," and others, which publish "U.S.S.R." in America. The Rockefellers also directly or indirectly financed the Coles Brothers' "Look magazine" and a chain of newspapers. They also financed a man named Sam Newhouse to buy up and build a chain of newspapers all over the country. And the late Eugene Myer, one of the founders of CFR, bought the "Washington Post," "Newsweek," the "Weekly magazine," and other publications.

At the same time, the CFR began to develop and nurture a new breed of scurrilous columnists and editorials writers such as Walter Lippman, Drew Pearson, the Alsops, Herbert Matthews, Erwin Canham, and others of that ilk who called themselves "Liberals" who proclaimed that "Amercanism" is "isolationism;" that "isolationism" is "war mongerism;" that "anti-communism" is "anti-semiticism" and "racism."

All that took time of course, but today our "weeklies," published by patriotic organizations, is completely controlled by CFR stooges and thus they finally succeeded in breaking us up into a Nation of quarreling, wrangling, squabbling, hating factions. Now if you still wonder about this slanted news and outright lies you read in your newspaper and watch on television, you now have the answer. To the Lehmans, Goldman-Sachs, Kuhn-Loebs, and the Warburgs, the CFR assigned the job of getting control of the motion picture industry, Hollywood, radio, and television, and believe me they succeeded.

If you still wonder about the strange propaganda broadcast by the late Ed

Morrows and others of that ilk, you now have the answer. If you wonder about all the smut, sex, pornography, and mixed marriage films you see in your movie theater and on your televison set (all of which is demoralizing our youth), you now have the answer.

Now to refresh your memory, let's go back for a moment. Wilson's flop had torpedoed all chances of transforming that "League of Nations" into what the conspirators had hope for, a one-world government housing. So the Jacob Schiff plot had to be done all over again and they organized the CFR to do it. We also know how successfully the CFR did that job of brainwashing and destroying the unity of the American people.

But, as was the case with the Schiff plot, the climax and the creation of a new housing for their one world government required another world war. A war that would be even more horrible and more devastating than the first world war in order to get the people of the world to again clamor for peace and a means to end all wars. But the CFR realized that the aftermath of World War II would have to be more carefully planned so that there would be no escape from the new one-world trap - another "League of Nations" that would emerge from the new war. The trap we now know as the "United Nations" and they hit upon a perfect strategy to ensure that no one escaped. Here is how they did it:

In 1943, in the midst of the war, they prepared the framework for the United Nations and it was handed over to Roosevelt and our State Department to be given birth by Alger Hess, Palvosky, Dalton, Trumbull, and other American traitors, thus making the whole scheme a United States' baby.

Then to fix our parenthood, New York City was to become the nursery for the monstrosity. After that we could hardly walk out on our own baby now could we? Anyway, that's how the conspirators figured it would work and so far it has. The liberal Rockefeller donated the land for the United Nations' building.

The United Nations' charter was written by Alger Hess, Palvosky, Dalton, Trumbull, and other CFR stooges. A phony, so-called, U.N. conference was set up in San Francisco in 1945. All the, so-called, representatives of 50-odd Nations gathered there and promptly signed the Charter and the despicable traitor, Alger Hess, flew to Washington with it elatedly submitted it to our Senate, and the Senate (elected by our people to safeguard our security) signed the Charter without so much as reading it. The question is "How many of our Senators were even then traitorous stooges of the CFR?" Anyway, it was thus that the people accepted the "United Nations" as a "holy of holies."

Again and again and again we have been startled, shocked, bewildered, and horrified by the UN's mistakes in Berlin, in Korea, in Laos, in Katanga, in Cuba, in Vietnam; mistakes that always favored the enemy, never the United States. Under the law of averages they should have made at least one or two mistakes in our favor, but they never did.

What's the answer? The answer is the "CFR" and the parts played by their subsidiaries and stooges in Washington D.C., thus we know that complete control of our foreign relation policy is the key to the success of the entire Illuminati one-world order plot. Here is further proof:

CHAPTER FOUR

Earlier I fully established that Schiff and his gang had financed the Lenin, Trotsky, Stalin, takeover of Russia and fashioned its communist regime into becoming their chief instrument to keep the world in turmoil and to finally terrorize all of us into seeking peace in a U.N. one-world government. But the conspirators knew that the "Moscow gang" could not become such an instrument until and unless the whole world would accept the communist regime as the legitimate "de jure government" of Russia.

Only one thing could accomplish that and that is the recognition by the United States. The conspirators figured that the whole world would follow our lead and that's their bag to induce Harding, Coolidge, and Hoover, to grant that recognition. But all three refused. As a result of the late 1920's, the Stalin regime was in dire straits. Despite all purges and secret police controls the Russian people were growing more and more resistive. It is a matter of record, admitted by Lipdenoff, that during 1931 and 1932 Stalin and his whole gang were always packed and ready for instant flight.

Then in November 1932, the conspirators achieved their greatest coup; they landed Franklin Roosevelt in the White House, crafty, unscrupulous, and utterly without conscience. That charlatan traitor turned the trick for them. Without even asking consent of Congress he unlawfully proclaimed recognition for the Stalin regime. That did it. And exactly as the conspirators figured the whole world did follow our lead. Automatically that squelched the previously growing resistance movement of the Russian people. That automatically launched the greatest menace the civilized world has ever known. The rest is too well known to need repeating.

We know how Roosevelt and his traitorous State Department kept building up the communist menace right here in our country and thus throughout the world. We know how he perpetuated the whole Pearl Harbor atrocity for his excuse to hurl us into World War II. We know all about his secret meetings with Stalin at Yalta and how he, with Eisenhower's help, delivered the

Balkans and Berlin to Moscow and last but by no means least, we know that the 20th century Benedict Arnold not only dragged us into that new corridor the United Nations, into the one-world government, but he actually schemed all the arrangements to plant it within our country.

In short, the day that Roosevelt entered the White House, the CFR conspirators regained full control of our foreign relations machinery and firmly established the United Nations as the housing for the Illuminati one-world government.

I wish to stress one other very vital point. That Wilson's "League of Nations" flop brought Schiff and his gang to the realization that control of just the Democratic Party was not enough.

True, they could create a crisis during the Republican administration as they did in 1929 with their Federal Reserve manufactured Crash and Depression which would bring another Democrat stooge back into the White House, but they realized that a four-year disruption in their control of our foreign relation policies could play havoc with the progress of their conspiracy. It could even break up their entire strategy as it almost did before Roosevelt saved it with his recognition of the Stalin regime.

Thereupon, after that Wilson debacle, they began to formulate plans to achieve control of both of our national parties. But that posed a problem for them. They needed manpower with stooges in the Republican Party with additional manpower for the Democratic Party and because control of just the man in the White House would not be enough, they would have to provide that man with trained stooges for his entire cabinet, men or women to head the State Department, the Treasury Department, the Pentagon, the CFR, the US Intelligence Agencies.

In short every member of the various cabinets would have to be a chosen tool of the CFR as well as all the under Secretaries and assistant Secretaries. That would give the conspirators absolute control of all our policies, both domestic and most important, foreign. That course of action would require a reserve pool of trained stooges instantaneously ready for administrative changes and for all other exigencies.

All such stooges would of necessity have to be people of national reputation, high in the esteem of the people, but they would have to be men and women without honor, without scruple, and without conscience. These people would have to be vulnerable to blackmail. It is needless for me to stress how well the CFR succeeded.

Now let's go back to the crux of the whole one-world government plot and the maneuvering necessary to create another "League of Nations" to house such a government.

As I have already stated, the conspirators knew that only another world war was vital for the success of their plot. It would have to be such a horrifying world war that the peoples of the world would cry out for the creation of some kind of a world organization that could secure an everlasting peace. But how could such a war be brought about? All the European nations were at peace. None had any quarrels with their neighboring nations and certainly their stooges in Moscow wouldn't dare to start a war. Even Stalin realized that it would mean the overthrow of his regime unless "patriotism" would weld the Russian people behind him.

But the conspirators had to have a war. They had to find or create some kind of an incident to launch it. They found it in a little inconspicuous and repulsive little man who called himself Adolf Hitler.

Hitler, an impecunious Austrian house painter had been a corporal in the German army. He made the defeat of Germany into a personal grievance. He began to rabble rouse about it in the Munich, Germany area. He began to spout about restoring the greatness of the German Empire and the might of the German solidarity. He advocated the restoration of the old German military to be used to conquer the whole world. Strangely enough, Hitler, the little clown that he was, could deliver a rabble rousing speech and he did have a certain kind of magnetism. But the new authorities in Germany didn't want anymore wars and they promptly threw the obnoxious Austrian house painter into a prison cell.

Aha! Here was the man, decided the conspirators, who, if properly directed and financed, could be the key to another world war. So while he was in prison they had Rudolph Hess and Hermann Goering write a book which they titled Mein Kompf and attributed the authorship to Hitler, exactly as Lipdenoff wrote Mission to Moscow and attributed the authorship to Joseph Davies, then our ambassador to Russia and a stooge of the CFR. In Mein Kompf the Hitler pseudo-author outlined his grievances and how he would restore the German people to their former greatness.

The conspirators then arranged for a wide circulation of the book among the German people in order to arouse a fanatical following for him. On his release from prison (also arranged by the conspirators), they began to groom and finance him to travel to other parts of Germany to deliver his rabble rousing speeches. Soon he gathered a growing following among other veterans of the war that soon spread to the masses who began to see in him a savior for their beloved Germany.

Then came his leadership of what he called "his brown shirt army" and the march on Berlin. That required a great deal of financing, but the Rothschilds, the Warburgs, and others of the conspirators provided all the money he needed. Gradually Hitler became the idol of the German people and they then overthrew the Von Hindenburg government and Hitler became the new Fuhrer. But that still was no reason for a war.

The rest of the world watched Hitler's rise, but saw no reason to interfere in what was distinctly a domestic condition within Germany. Certainly none of the other Nations felt it was a reason for another war against Germany and the German people were not yet incited into enough of a frenzy to commit any acts against any neighboring nation, not even against France that would lead to a war. The conspirators realized they would have to create such a frenzy - a frenzy that would cause the German people to throw caution to the winds and at the same time horrify the whole world. And incidentally, Mein Kompf was actually a follow-up of Karl Marx's book "A World without Jews".

The conspirators suddenly remembered how the Schiff- Rothschild gang had engineered the pogroms in Russia which slaughtered many, many thousands of Jews and created a world-wide hatred for Russia and they decided to use that same unconscionable trick to inflame the new Hitler-led German people into a murderous hatred of the Jews.

Now it is true that the German people never had any particular affection for the Jews, but neither did they have an ingrained hatred for them. Such hatred would have to be manufactured so Hitler was to create it. This idea more than appealed to Hitler. He saw in it the grisly gimmick to make him the "God-man" of the German people.

Thus craftily inspired and coached by his financial advisers, the Warburgs, the Rothschilds, and all the Illuminati masterminds, he blamed the Jews for the hated Versailles Treaty and for the financial ruination that followed the war. The rest is history. We know all about the Hitler concentration camps and the incineration of millions of Jews.

And here let me reiterate how little the internationalist bankers, the Rothschilds, Schiffs, Lehmans, Warburgs, Barouchs, cared about their racial brethren who were the victims of their nefarious schemes. In their eyes, the slaughter of innocent Jews by Hitler didn't bother them at all.

They considered it a necessary sacrifice to further their Illuminati one-world plot just as the slaughter of the many millions in the wars that followed was a similar necessary sacrifice. And here is another grisly detail about those concentration camps. Many of the Hitler soldier executioners in those camps had previously been sent to Russia to acquire their arts of torture and brutalization so as to emphasize the horrors of the atrocities.

All this created a new world-wide hatred for the German people but it still did not provide a cause for a war. There upon Hitler was incited to demand the "Sudetenland" and you remember how Chamberlain and the then diplomats of Czechoslovakia and France surrendered to that demand. That demand led to further Hitlerian demands for territories in Poland and in the French Czar Territories and those demands were rejected.

Then came his [Non-Aggression] pact with Stalin. Hitler had been screaming hatred against communism (Oh how he ranted against communism), but actually Nazism was nothing but socialism, and communism is, in fact, socialism. But Hitler disregarded all that. He entered into a pact with Stalin to attack and divide Poland between them. While Stalin marched into one part of Poland (for which he was never blamed [the Illuminati masterminds saw to that]); Hitler launched a "blitzkrieg" on Poland from his side. The conspirators finally had their new world war and what a horrible war it was.

And in 1945, the conspirators finally achieved the United Nations, their new housing for their one-world government. And truly amazing, all of the American people hailed this foul outfit as a Holy of Holies. Even after all the true facts about how the U.N. was created were revealed, the American people continued to worship that evil outfit. Even after Alger Hess was unmasked as a Soviet spy and traitor, the American people continued to believe in the U.N.

Even after I had publicly revealed the secret agreement between Hess and Mulatoff that a Russian would always be the head of the military secretariat and by that token, the real master of the U.N. But most of the American people continued to believe that the U.N. could do no wrong. Even after Trig D. Lee, the first Secretary general of the U.N. confirmed that Hess-Mulatoff secret agreement in his book: For The Cause of Peace, Vasialia was given a leave of absence by the U.N. so that he could take command of the North Koreans and Red Chinese who were fighting the so-called U.N. police action under our own General McArthur, who, by orders of the U.N., was fired by the pusillanimous president Truman in order to prevent him from winning that war.

Our people still believed in the U.N. despite our 150,000 sons who were murdered and maimed in that war; the people continued to regard the U.N. as a sure means for peace even after it was revealed in 1951 that the U.N. (using our own American soldiers under U.N. command, under the U.N. flag, in collusion with our traitorous State Department and the Pentagon) had been invading many small cities in California and Texas in order to perfect their plan for the complete takeover of our country. Most of our people brushed it off and continued their belief that the U.N. is a Holy of Holies.

Do you know that the U.N. Charter was written by traitor Alger Hess, Mulatoff, and Vyshinsky? That Hess and Mulatoff had made within that secret agreement that the military chief of the U.N. was always to be a Russian appointed by Moscow? Do you know that at their secret meetings at Yalta, Roosevelt and Stalin, at the behest of the Illuminati operating as the CFR, decided that the U.N. must be placed on American soil?

Do you know that most of the U.N. Charter was copied intact, word for word, from the Marx Communist Manifesto and the Russian, so-called, constitution? Do you know that the only two Senators who voted against the U.N. Charter had read it? Do you know that since the U.N. was founded, communist enslavement has grown from 250,000 to 1,000,000,000?

Do you know that since the U.N. was founded to insure peace there have been at least major wars incited by the U.N., just as they incited war against little Rhodesia and Kuwait? Do you know that under the U.N.

set up, the American taxpayers have been forced to make up the U.N. Treasury deficit of many millions of dollars because of Russia's refusal to pay her share? Do you know that the U.N. had never passed a resolution condemning Russia or her so-called satellites, but always condemns our Allies?

Do you know that J. Edgar Hoover said: "the overwhelming majority of the communist delegations to the U.N. are espionage agents" and that 66 Senators voted for a "Consular Treaty" to open our entire country to Russian spies and saboteurs? Do you know that the U.N. helps Russia's conquest of the world by preventing the free world from taking any action whatsoever except to debate each new aggression in the U.N. General Assembly?

Do you know that at the time of the Korean War there were 60 Nations in the U.N., yet 95% of the U.N. forces were our American sons and practically 100% of the cost was paid by the United States taxpayers?

And surely you know that the U.N. policy during the Korean and Vietnam Wars was to prevent us from winning those wars?

Do you know that all the battle plans of General McArthur had to go first to the U.N. to be relayed to Vasialia, Commander of the North Koreans and Red Chinese, and that any future wars fought by our sons under the U.N. flag would have to be fought by our sons under the control of the U.N. Security Council? Do you know that the U.N. has never done anything about the 80,000 Russian Mongolian troops that occupied Hungary?

Where was the U.N. when the Hungarian freedom fighters were slaughtered by the Russians [1956]. Do you know that the U.N. and its peace army turned the Congo over to the communists? Do you know that the U.N.'s own, so-called, peace force was used to crash, rape, and kill the white anti-communists in Katanga?

Do you know that the U.N. stood by and did nothing while Red China invaded Laos and Vietnam? That it did nothing while Nero invaded Goa and other Portuguese territories? Do you know that the U.N. was directly responsible for aiding Castro? That it does absolutely nothing about the many thousands of Cuban youngsters who are shipped to Russia for communist indoctrination.

Do you know that Adlai Stevenson said: "the free world must expect to loose more and more decisions in the U.N." Do you know that the U.N. openly proclaims that its chief objective is a "one-world government" which means "one-world laws," "one-world court," "one-world schools," and a "one world church" in which Christianity would be prohibited?

Do you know that a U.N. law has been passed to disarm all American citizens and to transfer all our armed forces to the U.N.? Such a law was secretly signed by saint' Jack Kennedy in 1961. Do you realize how that fits in with Article 47, paragraph 3, of the U.N. Charter, which states and I quote: "the military staff committee of the U.N. shall be responsible through the Security Council for the strategic direction of all armed forces placed at the disposal of the Security Council" and when and if all our armed forces are transferred to the U.N., your sons would be forced to serve and die under the U.N. command all over the world. This will happen unless you fight to get the U.S. out of the U.N.

Do you know that Congressmen James B. Utt submitted a bill to get the U.S. out of the U.N. and a resolution to prevent our President from forcing us to support the U.N. embargoes on Rhodesia? Well, he did and many people all over the country wrote to their representatives to support the Utt bill and resolution. Fifty Congressmen, spear headed by Schweiker and Moorhead of Pennsylvania, introduced a bill to immediately transfer all our armed forces to the U.N.? Can you imagine such brazen treason? Was your Congressman one of those 50 traitors? Find out and take immediate action against him.

Now do you know that the National Council of Churches passed a resolution in San Francisco which states that the United States will soon have to subordinate its will to that of the U.N. and that all American citizens must be prepared to accept it? Is your church a member of the National Council of Churches? In connection with that, bear in mind that God is never mentioned in the U.N. Charter and their meetings are never opened with prayer.

The creators of the U.N. stipulated in advance that there should be no mention of

God or Jesus Christ in the U.N. Charter or in its U.N. headquarters. Does your pastor subscribe to that? Find out! Furthermore, do you know that the great majority of the, so-called, Nations in the U.N. are anti-christianity and that the U.N. is a completely godless organization by orders of its creators, the CFR Illuminati. Have you heard enough of the truth about the Illuminati's United Nations? Do you want to leave your sons and our precious country to the unholy mercy of the Illuminati's United Nations?

If you don't, write, telegraph, or phone your Representatives and Senators that they must support a bill to get the U.S. out of the U.N. and the U.N. out of the U.S. Do it today, now, before you forget! It is the only salvation for your sons and for our country.

Now I have one more vital message to deliver. As I told you, one of the four specific assignments Rothschild gave Jacob Schiff was to create a movement to destroy religion in the United States with Christianity to be the chief target. For a very obvious reason the Anti defamation League wouldn't dare to attempt to do it because such an attempt could create the most terrible blood bath in the history of the world, not only for the ADL and the conspirators, but for the millions of innocent Jews.

Schiff turned that job over to Rockefeller for another specific reason. The destruction of Christianity could be accomplished only by those who are entrusted to preserve it, by the pastors, the men of the cloth.

As a starter, John D. Rockefeller picked up a young, Christian minister by the name of Dr. Harry F. Ward. Reverend Ward if you please. At that time he was teaching religion at the Union Theological Seminary. Rockefeller found a very willing Judas in this Reverend and thereupon in 1907, he financed him to set up the Methodist Foundation of Social Service and Ward's job was to teach bright young men to become, ministers of Christ and to place them as pastors of churches.

While teaching them to become ministers, the Reverend Ward also taught them how to subtlety and craftily preach to their congregations that the entire story of Christ was a myth to cast doubts on the divinity of Christ, to cast doubts about the virgin Mary, in short to cast doubts on Christianity as a whole. It was not to be a direct attack, but much of it to be done by crafty insinuation that was to be applied, in particular, to the youth in the Sunday schools.

Remember Lenin's statement: "give me just one generation of youth and I'll transform the whole world." Then in 1908; the Methodist Foundation of Social Service, which incidentally was America's first communist front organization, changed its name to the Federal Council of Churches. By 1950, the Federal Council of Churches was becoming very suspect so in 1950 they changed the name to the National Council of Churches.

Do I have to tell you more about how this National Council of Churches is deliberately destroying faith in Christianity? I don't think so, but this I will tell you. If you are a member of any congregation whose pastor and church are members of this Judas organization, you and your contributions are helping the Illuminati's plot to destroy Christianity and your faith in God and Jesus Christ thus you are deliberately delivering your children to be indoctrinated with disbelief in God and Church and which can easily transform them into atheists.

Find out immediately if your Church is a member of the National Council of Churches and for the love of God and your children, if it is, withdraw from it at once. However, let me warn you that the same destroying religion process has been infiltrated into other denominations. If you have seen the "Negro on Selma" and other such demonstrations, you have seen how the Negro mobs were led and encouraged by ministers (and even Catholic priests and nuns) who marched along with them.

There are many individual churches and pastors who are honest and sincere. Find one such for yourself and for your children. Incidentally, this same Reverend Harry F. Ward was also one of the founders of the American Civil Liberties Union, a notorious pro-communist organization. He was the actual head of it from 1920 to 1940. He also was a co-founder of the American League against War and Fascism which, under Browder, became the Communist Party of the United States.

In short, Ward's entire background reeked of communism and he was identified as a member of the communist party. He died a vicious traitor to both his church and country and this was the man John D. Rockefeller picked and financed to destroy America's Christian religion in accordance with the orders given to Schiff by the Rothschilds.

In conclusion I have this to say. You probably are familiar with the story of how one Dr. Frankenstein created a monster to do his will of destroying his chosen victims but how instead in the end, that monster turned on his own creator, Frankenstein, and destroyed him. Well, the Illuminati/CFR has created a monster called the United Nations (who is supported by their minority groups, the traitorous mass communications media, and the traitors in Washington D.C.) which was created to destroy the American people.

We know all about that many-headed hydra-monster and we know the names of those who created that monster. We know all their names and I predict that one fine day the American people will come fully awake and cause that very monster to destroy its creator. True! The majority of our people are still being brainwashed, deceived, and deluded by our traitorous press, TV, and radio, and by our traitors in Washington D.C., but surely by now enough is known about the U.N. to stamp out that outfit as a deadly poisonous rattlesnake in our midst.

My only wonder is: "what will it take to awaken and arouse our people to the full proof?" Perhaps this record [transcript] will do it. A hundred thousand or a million copies of this record can do it. I pray to God it will. And I pray that this record will inspire you, all of you, to spread this story to all loyal Americans in your community.

You can do it by playing or reading, it to study groups assembled in your homes, at meetings of the American Legion, the VFW, the DAR, all other civic groups and women's clubs, especially the women's clubs who have their sons lives at stake. With this record, I have provided you with the weapon that will destroy the monster. For the love of God, of our Country, and of your children, use it! Get a copy of it into every American home.

CHAPTER FIVE

Interview With Terry Melanson: Illuminati, Eugenics, "Sky-Eye" chips and more

The following interview was conducted by MAD, the Administrator of NWOWATCHER and co-host of the REVOLUTION RADIO program.

MAD: Terry, thanks for speaking with us today. I've been checking out your informative website on a regular basis for a few years now, and you've always got interesting updates and articles to share. First off, could you give us a little background on how you became interested in topics of the "New World Order", and what made you decide to start your own website exposing these pervasive conspiracies?

TM: Thanks for asking and allowing me to indulge.

My quest began a little more than 17 years ago through an intense study of Bible prophecy. For a few years I was really obsessed. I bought all the popular prophecy books on the market, watched Jack Van Impe and Peter LaLonde religiously, and looked for signs of the end of the world and the imminent return of Christ. I was convinced that we were living in the last days foretold in Daniel, Revelation, Ezekiel, Jeremiah and Isaiah.

Gradually, the material I got my hands on started to expand my scope of investigation. The turning point occurred, as it did for many, when I was given a small book called "None Dare Call it Conspiracy". I was hooked. My attention was now directed toward the machinations of the hidden ruling elite. Somehow it never occurred to me that if the Antichrist were to be revealed there would necessarily have to be a very powerful clique of financiers and well-placed insiders directing his ascendancy. When you start learning about the CFR, the Trilateral Commission, the Bilderbergs, Secret Societies and a nefarious/nebulous Illuminati - all the pieces fall into place. Even knowing that there truly is something akin to a shadow government (they certainly make no mention of it in school), how can you go on and not have it change you in a profound way?

I then began to wonder what else I had never been told about. So throughout the 90s I devoured hundreds of volumes, on every subject, from the occult to quantum mechanics, astrophysics to freemasonry and the mysteries, to mainstream history and hidden history, the paranormal and into other faiths and spiritual persuasions. A veritable hodge-podge of seemingly conflicting views of the world, I know, but I was on a mission: to reveal that which was hidden from view. I had no intention of specializing, conforming, or adhering to one belief system or another; I just soaked it all up like a sponge.

Then in 2000 I got wired. The Net opened up an infinite amount of possibilities and for someone who is a seeker of knowledge by nature, it was a revelatory experience. I taught myself HTML and set about building my own version of the ubiquitous web page on Geocities. Paul Joseph Watson was just starting out on Geocities at the time as well. Some of my favorite sites from those days were Too good

Reports, "Wake up America/Hardtruth," and CentrExNews - the latter being the site, for better or worse, which introduced Svali to alternative circles with a 13-part interview.

As I had created unique content from the beginning, traffic increased steadily and I finally made the plunge to my own domain in 2002.

MAD: Aside from the nice layout and 100's of articles you've meticulously posted regarding government corruption, secret societies, mind control and September 11th, one of the biggest things I'd recommend about CONSPIRACY ARCHIVE is your fine work detailing the many atrocities of the modern day Eugenics Movement. Most people are unaware that the United States was the first nation to promote this practice in the mainstream, forcibly sterilizing and castrating nearly 100,000 people between 1900-1940 because they were deemed "unfit to breed". While Hitler utilized this idea to its fuller extent, it was America that first implemented the heinous practices from sea to shining sea. The main inspiration for the scientific ideal of Eugenics was Sir. Francis Galton, who was also the cousin of Evolutionist Charles Darwin, and a firm believer in "Survival of the Fittest". The Eugenics Movement is a virtually invisible history and is deeply entwined with America's secret foundations. We can also add the massive Native American slaughter into this whole equation, and the widespread slavery of Africans. This is a fairly open question, but what are your thoughts regarding the topic of Eugenics? Do you believe it's still ingrained in the "Illuminati" mindset today, and is it important that more people become aware of the role Eugenics has played in U.S. history?

TM: You are correct; since 2004 when I started entering stories into my news database, there have been 120+ entries/links to articles expounding various facets of eugenics and population control. I have created a special page so your readers can view the collection for themselves. Surprisingly, a good deal of the stories I've linked to have come from the MSM. In recent years class action suits have been initiated, forcing governments to compensate those who've been sterilized against their will – thus the media has had no choice but to touch upon the eugenics movement (if only in a peripheral fashion). I have also published the incredible articles of Phil and

Paul Collins, who regularly recount the significance of the Malthusian/Darwinian/Eugenical sociocracy of the ruling class.

The oligarchs, the nobility and aristocrats, liken themselves as superior in every respect. "Blue blood" is considered pure or free from inferior lines. The very origin of the word eugenics itself stems from the Greek words "good" and "generation" or "wellborn". Francis Galton coined it himself, to denote controlled breeding for the purification of the human race. As you mentioned, Galton was a cousin of Darwin's; they shared the same grandparent: Erasmus Darwin (1731-1802), a Freemason and one of the founding members of the elite-scientific Lunar Society. Erasmus was the author of Temple of Nature and Zoönomia, or, the Organic Laws of Life, in which the basic outline of the theory of evolution can be discerned.

It is important to remember that evolutionary theory was originally couched in white race/Anglo-Saxon terms and gained acceptance through a western literate audience. The dominance and intelligence of the white race over the whole circumference of the earth, to them, was the single greatest sociological proof by which western man had demonstrated to the world its superiority and god-given right to rule. Combined with Malthusian population control, the power elite utilize evolution and eugenics as a weapon against the undesirables: the morons, imbeciles and lesser races.

Eugenics became a well-funded industry. As you know, seed money for research was heavily supplied by the Rockefeller Foundation, the Ford Foundation, prominent Skull and Bones families such as the Harrimans and Kelloggs, and most of the eastern WASP establishment. In England, those who would advance the study of eugenics were family names such as Darwin, Huxley, Dodge, Osborn, Keynes and Downs. Charles Darwin's own son, Major Leonard Darwin (1850-1943), was the Eugenics Society President from 1911-1928, an Honorary President from 1928-43, and an attendee of the 1921 Second International Congress of Eugenics in New York. In turn, Major Leonard Darwin's niece, Ruth Darwin, was on the 1931 Brock Committee, which came to the conclusion that compulsory sterilization was the right course of action for "undesirables".

Nothing has changed today. Frederick Osborn - founding member of the American Eugenics Society and co-founder with John D. Rockefeller III of the Population Council in 1953 - famously said: "Eugenic goals are most likely to be attained under a name other than eugenics." (The Future of Human Heredity, 1968, p. 104) Thus, the names of the various organizations have dispensed with the eugenic moniker in favor of more palatable titles. The American Eugenics Society (1926-1973) changed its name to the Society for the Study of Social Biology (1973-present). The American Eugenics Society had also published the journals Eugenical News (1939-53) and Eugenics Quarterly (1953-68); afterwards, the publication was conveniently renamed as Social Biology (1969-95). Ostensible "family planning" organizations, such as the Rockefeller-funded Population Council, still operate in much the same manner as originally intended – though, the "undesirables" are now represented by the over-populated poor in Africa, Asia, and Latin America. Birth control, abortion, and sterilization are still the tools of the eugenical trade. It's used strategically to reduce population, along with war, disease and famine.

MAD: Likewise, you're always pretty up to date with the emerging RFID (Radio Frequency Identification) predicament. What do you think of the connections that some people have implied, that this technology is in fact the 'Mark of the Beast'? For those who are still unaware, could you explain exactly how RFID works, and where do you see the future of RFID as heading if the Elites get their way?

TM: RFID and the Verichip has at least caused those who believe in the Bible to track its progress and report on it vigorously. This is a good thing. Whether it will actually fulfill prophecy I can't speculate – though now, for the first time, the possibility of a Mark of the Beast is a technological possibility. It's the Big Brother/Police State surveillance aspect of RFID and human implants that warrants my own "tracking" of the phenomenon. Close to 1300 related stories have been entered into the news database since 2004.

RFID is pretty simple. It is a small tag attached to products, livestock or humans which, when scanned with radio waves, emits unique identifying digital data. It is passive, in that the power supply is not contained with the tag or chip itself. It yields information only when scanned by a nearby reader. Thus, the range of tracking is very limited, down to feet.

With active RFID the chip would have its own power supply and emit a continuous signal, perhaps with the added capability of satellite tracking. The media will tell you that active RFID solutions are still in development and that it is years away yet. They forget, however, that it was one of their own who, in 1998, reported on a chip much more advanced than either Verichip or Digital Angel – indeed, one that was incredibly "active". The Sunday Times (London), 11 October 1998, sec. 1, p. 13, ran a story, "007 Implant to Protect Kidnap Targets," by reporters Maurice Chittenden and David Lloyd. It was a report about a company called Gen-Etics, who had produced a microchip implant called Sky-Eyes (based upon Mossad technology), trackable by satellite, and "made of 'synthetic and organic fiber'." The chip ran "on four milliamperes of neurophysiological energy."

007 implant to protect kidnap targets

THE SUNDAY TIMES (London)
by Maurice Chittenden and David Lloyd

THIS is the bleep that says: "Rescue me." A microchip under the skin that can help to locate hostages is being marketed to combat one of the world's biggest growth industries - there were a record 1,407 abductions for ransom worldwide last year, up 60% since 1990.

The victim's "little helper" uses natural body energy with James Bond-style technology devised by scientists working for Israeli intelligence.

Space satellites will follow the bleep to detect a victim's movements or hiding place. The information will then be relayed to a control center to be used for a rescue operation.

The device has come too late for three British engineers and a New Zealand colleague abducted in Chechnya last weekend. But film stars and the children of millionaires are among 45 people, including several Britons, who have been approached and fitted with the chips in secret tests during the past three months. The chips, costing £5,000 a time, are being launched in Milan this week.

However, kidnap experts are divided on whether the Sky-Eye chip is just another fashion accessory for the painfully rich or a valuable weapon in the fight against extortion.

The Gen-Etics company, which makes the chip, says it is being targeted at people in the public eye such as Leonardo DiCaprio, the Titanic star whose family originates from an area of southern Italy steeped in kidnapping, and companies that send employees to potentially dangerous places such as Colombia, Mexico and Chechnya. The company developed the chip for commercial use after it was invented by Mossad, the Israeli secret service, and used by agents on special missions.

Nicholas Ventura, in charge of marketing the device, said: "Film stars like DiCaprio and Robert De Niro are the kind of personalities this is aimed at - basically millionaires, VIPs and captains of industry who for family or work reasons go to places where kidnap gangs are active."

He refused to identify any clients. Customers on his doorstep could include the Duchess of York, who regularly visits the castle of Count Gaddo della Gherardesca, her Tuscan boyfriend; Sting, the rock star, who has a villa in Tuscany; and Greta Scacchi, the Anglo-Italian actress born in Milan.

The 43 Europeans and two Americans who have so far adopted the chip had surgery under a light anaesthetic. Gen-Etics claims the surgery is intended to daze the patient and prevent him or her remembering exactly where the incision was made, so he cannot reveal the chip's location to his abductors even under torture.

Every chip is made of synthetic and organic fibres and measures 4mm by 4mm. It does not need a battery and runs instead on four milliamperes of neurophysiological energy.

Only a small scar is visible and the chip escapes detection by x-rays. It is inserted under the skin but not on areas that can be amputated, including the hands, nose and ears.

Posting an earlobe to the family of a victim is a favorite technique for kidnap gangs. John Paul Getty III, grandson of the oil billionaire and one of 700 people kidnapped in Italy in the past 30 years, suffered such a fate in 1973.

The whereabouts of the carrier are followed by six satellites through the global positioning system, which has a 150-metre margin of error and has previously been used to track the movements of stolen luxury cars. The absence of a signal suggests that the victim has been killed because the body no longer supplies the energy to make the chip function.

The Sky-Eye is seen as an alternative to surrounding the children of the rich and famous with teams of burly bodyguards. Donatella Versace, sister of the murdered Italian fashion designer, appears to be well aware of the risks. Her two children, Allegra - who inherited the larger part of her uncle

Gianni's fortune - and Daniel, are watched over by a phalanx of security men whenever they step out of the family's 18th-century palazzo in Milan.

Others are more cynical about the microchip, however. Robert Davies, a special risks underwriter for Hiscox, an insurance group that holds 5,000 kidnap policies, said it might work in Britain or the United States but could prove hazardous in less developed countries, where victims were likely to be shot in rescue attempts and the police were sometimes in league with the kidnappers.

"We are aware that kidnap gangs in Mexico, the most sophisticated in the world, are searching victims for scars that might hide such devices. There is also the effect on morale if a victim thinks he will be quickly rescued but his family decides that would be a stupid thing to attempt," he said. Terry Waite, who was a hostage in Beirut for 5 1/2 years, said: "It is very dangerous because once kidnappers get to know about these things they will skin you alive to find them. There were rumors when I was kidnapped that I had been planted with locator devices.

"I was given rigorous searches, my clothes were changed and I even had my teeth checked."

The above story has been erased from the Sunday Times' website. Even the Wayback Machine's record of it has been expunged. (Both were there about 2 years ago, and when I started poking around and calling up the pages; they soon took care of that). The Chittenden and Lloyd story in the Sunday Times seems to be based upon a report in The Telegraph Journal a few days before.

Even Time Magazine couldn't resist:

A Secret Weapon to Thwart Kidnappers

Israeli scientists are marketing a microchip that, implanted under the skin, will protect film stars and millionaires from kidnap gangs. The chip emits a signal detectable by satellite to help rescuers determine a victim's approximate location. Originally developed to track Israeli secret-service agents abroad, the $5,000 battery-less Sky-Eye chip sold by Gen-Etics runs solely on the neurophysiological energy generated within the human body. Gen-Etics won't reveal where the chip is inserted but says 43 people have had it implanted.

The point is the public has been kept in the dark about current advances regarding implantable chips. The 1998 story made headlines briefly, in a few places, and was never repeated afterwards. Either the story was a hoax (in which case, let's see the retraction), or it has been covered up because too much was revealed. The Sky-Eyes chip was light years ahead of anything we see on the market today; 43 people had already been implanted, it could be detected by satellite, and was virtually unnoticeable, being partially constructed with organic fibers. Something like that has to be kept secret and out of the hands of the public, especially rival intelligence services.

MAD: Fascinating inclusions Terry, thanks for sharing those articles. Ironic that the pieces themselves have been "abducted" or "kidnapped" from the Web. I understand that you're currently writing a detailed expose on the history of the Bavarian Illuminati, headed under Professor Adam Weishaupt. Please, if you can share any details, could you give us a bit of a description for what this book will entail, and when might it be available to the public?

TM: It is a book long overdue in the English language. For 200 years reliable information on the Bavarian Illuminati has been sparse. The only histories in English are those of the Illuminists' contemporaries: John Robison, Proofs of a Conspiracy (1797) and Augustin Barruel, Memoirs Illustrating the History of Jacobinism (1798). Nothing substantial has subsequently been published. It's as if Robison and Barruel had written everything there was on the subject and further study was not even necessary.

As a consequence of this vacuum, more tall tales have been told about the ultimate bogey, the Illuminati, than any other subject. Legitimate study of the Bavarian Illuminati has been tainted because of the wild theories associated with the very word, "Illuminati." German scholarship, however, has continued unimpeded – it was, after all, their homeland in which the group had ascended. While research in English speaking countries was nonexistence, German professors were scouring the dusty archives throughout the entire continent of Europe. They have uncovered official lists of hundreds more confirmed members, doctoral theses have been written, and major studies have analyzed new material brought to light.

Some of this I reference, especially the definite lists of members. I've gone back and acquired copies of the Original Writings of the Illuminati for myself - representing the main primary material which both Robison and Barruel consulted - and read the definitive history of the Order: René Le Forestier's 1914 Les Illuminés de Bavière et la franc-maçonnerie allemande. Rounding out the research are stacks of books regarding all aspects of the European Enlightenment. My basement is starting to resemble a well-stocked history section of a university library.

With the lists of initiates as a stating point, I've written biographies of over four-hundred of them. Barruel, for instance, writing as a contemporary in the late 1790s, had sparse information. At most he had identified about eighty members, and only in a cursory manner: name, and/or occupation, and/or alias etc. – that was the extent of it. With the hindsight of 200 years of history and hundreds more membership confirmations, the time is ripe to re-write the entire history, purpose, and significance of the Order for an English audience.

The new book, Perfectibilists: The 18th Century Bavarian Order of the Illuminati, is almost finished and will be available in most major outlets. Nothing but the facts in this one, but written from the perspective of one who actually believes in the reality of a "conspiracy theory." I think of it as the book that Antony Sutton always wanted to write but never had the chance. As a tribute, I include a bit of speculation near the end, which expands upon circumstantial connections to the Skull and Bones. Sutton thought – and rightly so - that there was a real possibility that S&B were the heirs or second branch of the original Bavarian Illuminati. I have uncovered even more evidence that seems to suggest this.

MAD: Sounds like it will be a very interesting and important read, Terry. Regarding you new book, you've also revealed that you have a fairly long and detailed list of members who were involved in the 1776 Illuminati, and other organizations which they also might have belonged to. Who are some of the more prominent individuals whom were known to have, or believed to have belonged to, Weishaupt's Illuminati? Also, since Weishaupt was once a member of the group, how do you think the Vatican's Jesuit Order ties into the possible birth of the Illuminati? (In terms of the Skull and Bones society of which you mention, and both John Kerry and George W. Bush were members, we also have the connection that new initiates into this order are inducted by a hooded 'Don Quixote' figure, and that Quixote author, Miguel de Cervantes, also Jesuit trained, stated that the character was loosely based upon the first Superior General of the Jesuit Order, Ignatius Loyola.) [A Don Quixote/Jesuit Relation]

TM: Let me address your last statement/question first. Weishaupt was educated by the Jesuits, it is true, just as most of the middle class, bourgeoisie, or even the nobility at the time in Bavaria. He was not one of them, however. Weishaupt had only attended Jesuit-controlled schools during his formative years. The Jesuits had a monopoly on education throughout the whole of Catholic Europe; Protestant realms weren't free from their influence either.

The Jesuits were suppressed by the Pope in 1773. During this year, at Ingolstadt University, Weishaupt was already a tenured professor of civil law and was subsequently appointed to the vacant chair of canon law – the first time occupied by a non-Jesuit in 80 years. Many of the Jesuit professors at Ingolstadt continued to teach afterwards – there just weren't many others who had the qualifications. Weishaupt's appointment enraged the "former-Jesuits". A fight ensued and Weishaupt was targeted for investigation: procuring "ungodly" books for the University library, among other things. He was continuously hounded, and he never forgot his ill treatment.

When Weishaupt founded his Order in 1776, it was in large part as a mechanism in which to counter the absolutism of the Jesuits. Throughout the Illuminati's existence they fought the Jesuits tooth and nail. They even invested in their own printers, producing and widely distributing copies of anti-Jesuit material. All the top members of the Illuminati were seasoned and skilled Jesuit hunters! Most of them published their own books attacking the Jesuits in every manner conceivable – which was a main reason they were recruited to begin with. Freemasons and Illuminati were dead serious in their struggle against the very real threat of Jesuit hegemony. The conspiracy industry was born out of it. Before the ubiquitous screed against the threat of the Illuminati - pamphlets, books and monographs decried the menace of Jesuit maniacal world control.

I had to get that off my chest. In conspiracy circles, Jesuits and Illuminati have been become synonymous of late and it is a fallacy to suggest that they are – or were – one and the same. I can back up that statement, while I know for a fact those in the Jesuit-Illuminati camp cannot.

The references to Cervantes' Don Quixote in the Skull and Bones initiations most likely stem from a keen reading of Laurence Sterne's The Life and Opinions of Tristram Shandy (1759-67). The most important figure in the SB initiations is that of Uncle Toby. They take turns being called "Uncle Toby", he directs the entire proceeding, and indeed is the master of everything that takes place within the Tomb on a day to day basis. Uncle Toby is one of the prime characters in Tristram Shandy.

Sterne was educated by the Jesuits (probably was one himself), and was a priest and deacon. The religious satirical writing of Alexander Pope (Essays on Man, 1734) and Cervantes, was Sterne's main influence for the incredibly popular satire which is Tristram Shandy. Sterne even references Don Quixote's horse in the novel, Rocinante. The comic (bawdy humor) English novel in the 18th Century constantly referenced Quixote - in fact Cervantes had created the genre.

I don't usually quote from Wikipedia, but here's a good explanation of the influence I'm talking about:

The shade of Cervantes is ... present throughout Sterne's novel. The frequent references to Rocinante, the character of Uncle Toby (who resembles Don Quixote in many ways) and Sterne's own description of his characters' 'Cervantic humour,' along with the genre-defying structure of Tristram Shandy, which owes much to the second part of Cervantes' novel, all demonstrate the influence of Cervantes.

Here's where it gets interesting. Laurence Sterne's Tristram Shandy was explicitly recommended to Illuminati initiates! I have a whole section of one chapter in my book which goes into the details on exactly what authors and books were required reading for members. Now, the Illuminati cribbed liberally from all aspects relating to the Jesuits, but that's beside the point. The direct line I believe is Cervantes > Sterne > Illuminati > Skull and Bones. Along with many other circumstantial pieces, the fact that Uncle Toby is as prevalent within S&B life as it is, may have a lot to do with the Illuminati's original respect for Tristram Shandy to begin with. Reading Sterne, then, one can immediately discern the influence of Don Quixote on the latter as well - even by Sterne's own admission. So, they decided to enhance the "ceremonies" with additional sub-characters gleaned from Cervantes.

On to membership ... I really don't know where to start. I don't want to reveal too much either.

In general, much study was done on the lives of Mozart and Beethoven. Why? Because according to the substantial lists uncovered over the years, nearly all of their friends and acquaintances were Illuminati.

Not just Freemasons – as many have known for awhile, even Mozarts' affiliation with the latter – but major members of the Illuminati. Reading works on the life of Mozart, especially, is to learn the history of a powerful clique of Illuminati, mostly in and around Vienna. His patrons, his friends, his Freemasonic buddies: now confirmed members of the Illuminati. The significance of this is open to debate, but the mere fact that this history hasn't been told is enough for me.

The most informative part of the membership bios is the length to which I document the importance of pedagogy to the Illuminati. Sutton has written about it, and identified Pestalozzi and Wundt as the most influential. Basically, the educational techniques exported to the North American continent during the 19th century were not only traceable to members of the Illuminati, but they are methods of control being practiced within the Minerval lodges of the society itself. All members were tested with the techniques, and it made a lasting impression on them. It wasn't that Pestalozzi et al had discovered it by themselves; they had learned it through association with the Illuminati. (As for

Pestalozzi, I back up this assertion by quoting letters he sent before and after his initiation). The main goal of the Illuminati was to institute and control an educational empire for the indoctrination of the young. It worked, and still does. Books like The Deliberate Dumbing Down of America and The Underground History of American Education go into the details. Charlotte Thomson Iserbyt and John Taylor Gatto aren't experts on the history of the Illuminati, however - they didn't realize the true extent of what they had found.

MAD: You cover a variety of other so-called 'secret societies' on your site. Tell me, what are some of the other groups that your research indicates are the most powerful and influential in the orchestration of the New World Order within global events?

TM: The goal of the "New World Order" has been touted throughout the 20th Century within the context of, or relating too, control through the implementation of some form of world government. Round Table Group members have been the purveyors of such a plan. Collectively, this is where the pinnacle of power rests today. So, the most influential groups worthy of in-depth study are The Pilgrims, the Council on Foreign Relations, the Trilateral Commission, the Bilderberg Group, and the Royal Institute of International Affairs. It's as simple as that. The people who have the most overlap between these groups are the real controllers of us all. A CFR member might very well be a Zionist (Jewish or Christian), a Jesuit or a Freemason – perhaps all of the above. At this level it is irrelevant. They have chosen to consort among the power elite and consensus is required for the good of the whole. That's as monolithic as it gets, but it still involves different ideologies and a wide range of competing interests.

MAD: Do you believe that the classic "Illuminati" still exists today, and if so, who do you think might have membership with this all-encompassing group? How do the bloodline families play into this whole structure, the Pope and the President?

TM: It is highly unlikely that the 18th Century Bavarian Illuminati exists in any tangible form. From Weishaupt the mantle passed to JJC Bode, and after Bode died in Dec. 1793 the original Order seems to have vanished from history. Illuminist Duke Ernst II of Saxe-Gotha (1745-1804) - and his family afterwards - was the protector of Weishaupt for his entire life. The Duke had also inherited the papers of Bode. The House of Saxe-Gotha thus became the sole heir of all that was operational pertaining to the Illuminati. If the Illuminati had survived, it would be through the Royal House of Saxe-Gotha, later Saxe-Coburg-Gotha. Duke Ernst II's direct descendants sit on the throne of England (they changed their name from Saxe-Coburg-Gotha to the House of Windsor in 1917).

Perhaps the Illuminati morphed and became a purely aristocratic secret society, carrying on in a fashion akin to the Order of the Garter or the Order of the Golden Fleece. A great number of original members of the Illuminati also belonged to these same chivalric systems, so there are solid connections already. In this respect, it is not all that mysterious to contemplate hereditary perpetuation of a secret as dangerous as this. It may well have been the safest means to continue, making it very hard for outsiders to poke around thereafter. If this is the case then the original concept of Weishaupt's Illuminati may have coalesced and found a home within the more traditional knightly, "noble orders". Thus, "Bloodlines of the Illuminati" would be an acceptable description of reality.

MAD: Speaking of the President, you might have noticed that from both sides of the fake paradigm, controlled opposition election climate, we have Obama, Clinton, Edwards and Giuliani all showing fervent support for the protection and growth of Israel. Please tell me a little bit about your thoughts on how Zionism and Israel ties into this whole scenario, as well as how this might relate to Biblical prophecy, and corrupt racial superiority ideals in Hebrew texts such as the Talmud.

CHAPTER SIX

Candidates Court Israel

Obama-Strong Israel Supporter

TM: Not to downplay your question, but I'm against all "isms". Zionism, Talmudism, Kabbalism, Whahabism, Jesuitism, Illuminatism, Communism, Anarchism, Nihilism, Fabianism, Neo-conservatism, and Internationalism – even the more pleasant-sounding ones: they all represent a line drawn in the sand. Ideology is an excuse, the ultimate expression of which is cultism and zealotry.

Dialectics is what it's all about. Competing systems are necessary; if no opposite of an ideology is apparent, the reverse is manufactured accordingly. Of the pernicious isms mentioned above, they all stem from secret societies and are intended to divide the masses through social manipulation. "Ahh, you're a Jew – have I got something for you!" "Ooh, you're a

Muslim – the Imam al-Ummah has something you need to hear!" "What, you're a disenfranchised worker, you hate your boss and think there is something inherently wrong with capitalism – come right this way and meet my friend named Marx!"

In the US and Canada, yes, the Jewish lobby is exceedingly influential. Politicians conciliate, rather than risk being tagged an anti-Semite – a fate worst than death. There's also a higher tier of control at work. "Political correctness" encompasses Zionist aspirations just as it does for other ostensibly disenfranchised groups. The PC business is a behemoth Orwellian control mechanism, touching the lives of everyone. The prosecution of Thought-crimes has the same effect whether it is initiated by the SS, the Inquisition or the ADL.

MAD: Are there any candidates you would vote for, or does it seem that Voter Fraud is too rampant to even take American politics seriously anymore? Do you think there is ample evidence to prove that the elections were stolen in favor of Bush in both 00 and 04, and are they flaunting their power in front of our faces by having two

Skull and Bones members (Bush/Kerry) as candidates in the last election?

TM: Well, I'm Canadian so that pretty much settles the question! If I were American and had a chance I would vote for any party beside the big two; maybe libertarian or independent, but definitely no to the Jackass or Elephant variety. If Ron Paul were to run I'd definitely give him a chance.

As for the last question, the answer is yes, and yes. Election fraud should be punishable by a penalty equivalent to murder. It is a crime that serious.

MAD: Pardon me for my next question but I have to bring it up. You also have a section on your website dedicated to UFO's and cases of abductions, cattle mutilations and crop circles (which you state as being the most conjecture based information available). Briefly, what are some of your thoughts and theories on UFO phenomena? While I believe there is something to it all, I also think that at least half of the reports are hoaxes, and much of it is based largely on government techniques of psyops and propaganda, with a sprinkling of 'New Age' fairy dust.

TM: I'm glad you've brought this up. Though it is still accessible, the section has mostly remained dormant since 2001 (carried over from my Geocities days). I've received more than a few emails over the years admonishing me to forgo the "bunk," lest it discredit the rest of the site. I can see their point, and in many respects it is valid. However, those people who dismiss outright, or cringe at such study, probably never have experienced a single mystical or unexplained/paranormal occurrence. I've seen two UFOs in my life, and one of them was willed into existence – explicitly and clearly observed by myself and another for an extended period. It was an experiment, and it worked. This ties in directly with the occult; I was way in over my head with it at the time. When I look back on it now, the only explanation I can give is that it was a powerful demonstration of the validity of magic.

In general, my interest in UFOs is from the standpoint of comparative mythology, and in particular how it is similar to other phenomena of a paranormal/occult nature. I don't dwell on it too much anymore but then again strange things of an occult or paranormal nature haven't happened to me in quite some time. I'm actually going to redesign my site soon – when time permits – and I am seriously contemplating the deletion of (at least unlinking to) those archives entirely. I'm no Jacques Vallee or John Keel. And besides, Jeff Wells covers that area much better than I can.

MAD: What are some of your thoughts on the "Reptilian Agenda" that is popularly promoted by some authors today? What do you think of Sitchin, who helped to fuel this debate?

TM: Regarding bloodsucking, shapeshifting Alien Reptoids: I get emails from crazy people on a daily basis. I usually read it, chuckle, and carry on without a reply. I could make a quick buck if I ever decided to exploit them.

On Sitchin: Michael Heiser has said it much better and with greater authority than anyone on the entire planet: http://www.sitchiniswrong.com/

MAD: You've got a lot of great audio and video downloads available at CONSPIRACY ARCHIVE. Are there any books/documentaries that you would specifically recommend to readers today?

TM: Though the works cited are authoritative, this is not meant to be an exhaustive list. The subjects themselves reflect my own taste and areas of interest.

Bavarian Illuminati: Forestier, Les Illuminés de Bavière et la franc-maçonnerie allemande (si vous parle français) or Vol. 3 and 4 of Barruel's Memoirs Illustrating the History of Jacobinism.

Freemasonry: I would recommend scholarly research by Masons themselves. Seek out old copies of Ars Quatuor Coronatorum on eBay or Abebooks or even the Scottish Rite's The New Age Magazine. The former publication is coveted by historians and is of a quality equal to, in some cases surpassing that found in an academic journal. The Transactions of the Quatuor Coronati Lodge has traced the history, beliefs, practices and symbolism of Freemasonry and other occult groups with irrefutable accuracy. There are quite revealing things to be found in publications such as these.

Secret Societies and Occult Conspiracy: Charles William Heckethorn, Secret Societies of All Ages and Countries; Frances Yates, The Rosicrucian Enlightenment; Christopher McIntosh, The Rose Cross and the Age of Reason and his The Rosicrucians: The History, Mythology, and Rituals of an Esoteric Order; James Webb, The Occult Underground and The Occult Establishment.

Jewish mysticism, Kabbalah and Frankism: Gershom Scholem, Kabbalah his Sabbatai Sevi: The Mystical Messiah, 1626-1676 and his Major Trends in Jewish Mysticism; Jacob Katz, Jews and Freemasons in Europe 1723-1939; Arthur Mandel, Militant Messiah: Or, the Flight from the Ghetto: The Story of Jacob Frank the Frankist Movement; Marvin S. Antelman, To Eliminate the Opiate, Vol. I and II.

The Enlightenment (imperative to understanding the politics and beliefs of the modern western world): Reinhart Koselleck, Critique and Crises: Enlightenment and the

Pathogenesis of Modern Society; Klaus Epstein, The Genesis of German Conservatism; R. R Palmer, The Age of the Democratic Revolution II; Richard Van Dulmen, The Society of the Enlightenment; Nicholas Till, Mozart and the Enlightenment; G. Adolph Koch, Republican Religion: The American Revolution and the Cult of Reason.

Revolutionary movements: James H. Billington, Fire in the Minds of Men: Origins of the Revolutionary Faith; Elizabeth L. Eisenstein, The First Professional Revolutionist: Filippo Michele Buonarroti, 1761-1837; John Murray (trans.), Memoirs of the Secret Societies of the South of Italy, particularly the Carbonari; Nesta Webster, World Revolution and her Secret Societies and Subversive Movements.

Elite Social Control: Philip and Paul Collins, The Ascendancy of the Scientific Dictatorship; E. Michael Jones, Libido Dominandi: Sexual Liberation and Political Control.

MAD: This has been a fascinating and informative discussion Terry, and again, thanks so much for giving me some time today, I really appreciate it. I'll definitely keep checking out the Archive, and am looking forward to reading your new book. Here's wishing you much success in the publication, and hope we can keep in touch as things just keep getting curiouser and curiouser. As we finish up, are there any other parts to the puzzle that you'd like to reveal today, and any special messages you'd like to give to our readers?

TM: Thanks for the opportunity. I haven't been in the Nwowatcher forums for awhile but if anyone has comments or questions I'd be happy to reply.

I have included this interview in this book because it gives added information concerning the Illuminati – the people who control governments and economies. Information is vital to understanding the enemy. Understanding the enemy could very well produce a person, more intelligent than me, that will create a plan to foil the New World Agenda. Somewhere out there is such a person.

CHAPTER SEVEN

The Illuminati Inspect Every Hollywood Script:

DETECTING AND UNDERSTANDING ILLUMINATI INTERFERENCE

A scene from "V is for Vendetta" -- "The most blatantly honest Illuminati project I have yet viewed."

The Illuminati exert influence in popular visual media to an extraordinary extent. Every major film script that is in pre-production mode is submitted to key

Illuminati subordinates whose role is to assess the script for potential alterations or insertions. These changes may be major or minor, depending on the material of the script.

Additionally, these subordinates comprise a tightly managed think tank which surveys the progress of Illuminati propaganda in global societies. The members make decisions about which themes are ready for further amplification in popular media. Then, detailed descriptions of desired creative projects are handed down to a further subordinate (but not necessarily knowledgeable) group of highly skilled writers, who create the scripts for these projects.

Different projects are created to target different sectors of the global population. That may seem logically obvious, but it's worth stating. Grossly blatant Illuminati messages are more often couched in films of excessive violence, sexual content, outright weirdness, and so on, in order to distract viewers from the fact that external ideas are being inserted forcefully into their minds.

Actually, that's not quite right: excessive violence, and such, activates a psychological openness to the receiving of ideas. The explanation for this is that once a viewer makes the decision to ACCEPT the violence and the sex, and so on, his or her mind remains open to the ideas that the film is meant to insert into their minds.

SUBTLE INFLUENCES

Very often, the decision is made not to insert any open messages into film projects. This is due to two very simple rules: too much openness exposes the process; and, gradual influence is far more powerful and effective in the long run. In the event that no open messages are going to be inserted, two other options remain which still allow for gradual influence to build.

The first is Signature Symbology. The Illuminati have, over time, generated a huge set of symbols and visual icons which, in partnership with the more blatant messages, exert an impressive (some would say frightening) measure of influence on public thought.

These are the Signatures of Illuminati interference in a project. When viewers see a symbol inserted into a film, this event draws up memories of past encounters with that symbol, and of any messages or themes attached to that symbol.

This is often what some people call an "unconscious" or "subliminal" process. I call it "unreflective", for the simple reason that most people are just not paying any attention to the influences that affect them deeply.

Of course everyone wants to leap on the "Illuminati eye" as a blatantly repetitive symbol these days. That's a misguided judgment, and I'll get to that part soon. An example of a less obvious Signature Symbol is the gargoyle. Any film or other production featuring even brief glimpses of gargoyles is announcing that it has the Illuminati stamp of approval.

The second option is influence over the music attached to a project. Film music - well, music in general - holds a powerful influence over viewers and listeners. Similar musical themes across various projects excite unreflective (or subliminal) memories even more deeply than do visual symbols.

One of the tactics of the Illuminati is to present a large set of what we could call Distraction Symbols. The very name "Illuminati" is itself a Distraction Symbol. Distraction Symbols are meant to occupy the attention of both the mildly curious thinkers and the overly excitable conspiracy theorists.

Oftentimes, Distraction Symbols are in fact genuine signature symbols, but the publicly presented meanings of these symbols are well-planned and tightly controlled propaganda. The meanings of Distraction Symbols have been either completely falsified or else skewed just enough to push amateur analysts in the wrong directions.

Let's ask some questions. What do the Illuminati wish to accomplish? What do the subordinate participants in Illuminati projects wish to accomplish? What are the major themes the Illuminati focus on presenting? Why have they selected these particular themes?

WHO ARE ILLUMINATI?

There is no actual body of persons calling themselves the Illuminati. There DOES exist an actual body of persons telling everyone to CALL them "the Illuminati", but this is not what they call themselves. Nor is their character equal to the propaganda they have sponsored that purportedly describes "the Illuminati".

The most blatantly honest Illuminati project I have yet viewed is V for Vendetta, directed by Jon Turtletaub, starring Natalie Portman and Hugo Weaving. By the way, all three of these people are key production elements in major and obvious Illuminati film projects.

There is a scene in V for Vendetta where the central figures of the film, a man dressed in black and wearing a smiling mask (a Guy Fawkes mask, you can look it up, or watch the film), and a woman named Evie (after Eve, the symbolic Mother of Humankind), perform the following exchange:

Evie: How strange that I suddenly see your face everywhere.... I don't understand.

V: What?

Evie: How you can be one of the most important things that has ever happened to me, and yet I know almost nothing about you. I don't know where you were born, who your parents were, if you had any brothers or sisters... I don't even know what you really look like.

V: There is a face beneath this mask, but it's not me. I am no more that face than the muscles beneath it, or the bones beneath that.

This is Illuminatis' admission that their public representation of themselves is a very deliberate sham. They have intended all along to keep their membership, their ultimate intentions, and their core character as hidden as necessary. Therefore, if we examine what they present in overly forceful ways, we can discover what they are not.

Conversely, if we examine their more subtle touches, we can discover what they are willing to admit to - that is, what they MUST admit to, in order to build the future they have planned for Humanity.

Here we come to the issue of SEEDING. This is it. This is what Illuminati influence in public media is all about. The Illuminati are - like it or not - causing and controlling change, globally, but they are not doing that only by means of instigating economic crises and violent international conflicts.

The Illuminati are seeding the public with notions that gradually grow larger and more influential over time. They did it with Feminism; they did it with flexi-sexuality; they are doing it with anti-religion and with child sexualization now. They do this because the future society they have planned must be structured differently from what we all know now. A different structure requires citizens with different thinking who will accept that structure.

The Hollywood Kabbalah Club Unmasked:

Jay Z, Rihanna, Bono, and Lady Gaga demonstrate their allegiance to the Kabbalah cult, also known as the Illuminati.

If you ever wondered why the lives of Hollywood stars are so troubled but concluded the reason was nothing more than vanity, substance abuse, and too much money, think again.

Hollywood is ruled by a Kabbalistic cult—also known as the Illuminati—which is wreaking havoc in the lives those on the silver screen and in the music industry, according to blogger 101 The Destroyer in The Wake Up series.

The Destroyer has created a series of videos shedding light on Hollywood's deep dark secret, and all the big names are implicated. MK Ultra mind control, ritual murder, witchcraft, Freemasonry, membership at the Kabbalah Center, and selling one's soul to the devil are not the exception to the rule to making it in Hollywood but are actually prerequisites.

The proof: The prevalence of dissociative identity disorder (also known as split personality disorder) among the stars and their obsessive use of hand signs and occult symbolism in their album art, and in their on-stage theatrics. Then there are the red Kabbalah bracelets that Hollywoodites can be found wearing when they are out of character.

But I am going to let the video presentations do the talking. I have broken down the main points from each of the 42 videos in point form below. The first nine videos are rather dry if you are an avid conspiracy researcher. The good stuff starts at about Part 10. Part 14, where ex-Illuminatus John Todd reveals that every record album produced has a spell cast on it by witches, is the most interesting video out of the entire series in my opinion. The rest reveal some very interesting, little-known facts and piece everything together.

Out of all of the stars examined in The Wake Up series, you will learn that Madonna and Lady Gaga are two of the most loyal followers of Lucifer, and they are not afraid to admit it. Many of the other stars are not so loyal, and when they start to rebel from their childhood-based Illuminati programming or renege on their unspoken contract with Hollywood devils, they wind up dead or demoted. I guess Randy Quaid isn't crazy after all.

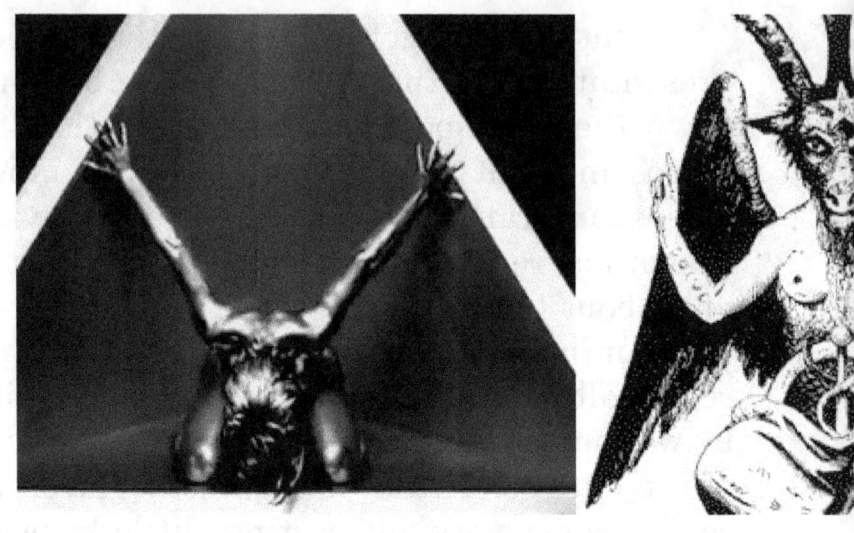

Rhianna bent over inside a pyramid in the Umbrella music video. The videographers obviously doctored this scene to extend Rhianna's neck—creating the snout—and to create the eyes at her shoulders—stylized after the Baphomet head on the right. In real time, this particular scene flashes by rather quickly to give it a subliminal effect. Rihanna doing her Baphomet thing again:

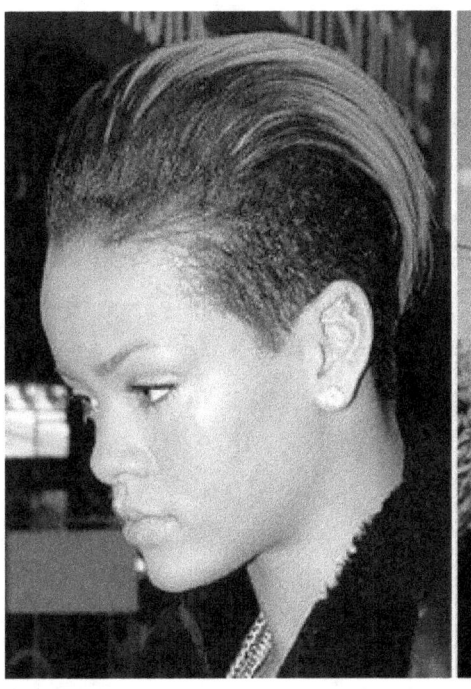

It is extremely important to monitor the movies and musical videos your children watch. Hollywood and the Illuminati are out to steal and corrupt their minds.

The Illuminati Conspiracy against God:

Have you noticed? Each year, there is a little less Christ in Christmas, a little less Christian spirit. The spirit of giving now is confined to gifts. Scarcely is there mention of

Christian love. That might offend some people, Satanists perhaps.

God is Love. Satanists aren't big fans of Love. They have a lot of clout.

Incredible and bizarre as it sounds, a Satanic cult, the Illuminati rules the world. George W. Bush is a member, as is much of the present world's political and economic elite.

The Illuminati consist of some of the world's richest families including the Rothschilds, the Rockefellers and the Windsors. While they pay lip service to religion, they worship Lucifer. Their agents control the world's media, education, business and politics. These agents may think they are only pursuing success, but success literally means serving the devil. Prisoners of their wealth, the Illuminati prefer hatred and destruction to Love. Understandably, they can't go public with this. They pretend to be moral while working behind the scenes to degrade and enslave humanity in a "new world order."

Hiroshima, Dresden, Auschwitz,

Cambodia and Rwanda were sacrifices to their god Lucifer. They are responsible for the two World Wars, the Depression and the Cold War. Sept. 11, the War on Terror and the Iraq Wars are their latest achievements.

We imagine they want unlimited power and wealth but these are by-products. The Illuminati is motivated by hatred of God and humanity.

OUR LUCIFER-LOVING ELITE

The purpose of the New World Order is the same as Communism. The Illuminati created Communism as a means to flaunt God's will and enslave mankind. Karl Marx was hired to sell totalitarian rule ("the dictatorship of the proletariat"). Marx duped the masses by pretending to espouse equality. He was a Satanist as were Trotsky, Lenin and Stalin.

In his book, 'Marx and Satan'(1986) Richard Wurmbrand illustrates Marx`s true hatred of God and humanity. As early as 1848, Marx wrote about a "coming world war" that will eliminate "riffraff" like Russians, Czechs and Croats.

"The coming world war will cause not only reactionary classes and dynasties, but also entire reactionary peoples to disappear from the face of the earth. And that will be progress...the revolution...cares as little about the human lives it destroys ...as an earthquake cares about the houses it ravages. Classes and races that are too weak to dominate the new conditions ...will be defeated...their very name will vanish. "

In his poem "Human Pride" Marx writes that he will "wander Godlike and victorious through the ruins of the world...I will feel equal to the Creator.

Far from a champion of the working class, Marx was a Satanist and a sociopath. He was also a spy for the Austrian police. In 1960, the Austrian Chancellor Raabe gave Khrushchev an original letter by Marx proving the founder of Communism informed on other revolutionaries.

The reason only 13 of the 100 Volumes of Marx's writings have been published is to hide the true character of Communism.

THEY HATE THE GOD IN YOU

Wurmbrand, a pastor who was imprisoned in Romania, says Communism is in essence Satanism empowered. Christians weren't just brutally persecuted and murdered, they were made to blaspheme. Communism's goal is to mock God and to praise Lucifer. A Communist newspaper confessed, ""We fight against God: To snatch believers from him."

In "German Ideology" Marx referred to God in Hegelian terms as the Absolute Spirit. Marx opined, "we are concerned with a highly interesting question: the decomposition of the Absolute Spirit."

According to Wurmbrand, the Russian Revolution was a time when love, goodwill, and healthy feeling were considered mean and retrograde. A girl hid her innocence, and husbands their faithfulness. Destruction was praised as good taste, neurasthenia as the sign of a fine mind. This was the theme of new writers who burst on the scene out of obscurity. Men invented vices and perversion, and were fastidious in their avoidance of being thought moral.

The Luciferians portray their rebellion against God and nature as "progress and freedom." This permissiveness refers only to tearing down the Divine and natural order. In the initiation into the Seventh degree of Satanism, the adept swears, Nothing is true and everything is permitted. In the Communist Manifesto, Marx said all religion and morals will be abolished and everything permitted.

The religion of modern western society, secular humanism, is Illuminism (Lucifer worship in disguise.)

The purpose of Illuminism is to divorce humanity from the Divine Purpose and enshrine Lucifer (i.e. the Illuminati) in God`s place. Under the guise of a humanist utopia, they are constructing an Orwellian hell -- the New World Order.

The goal of globalism is the same as Communism. The world`s elite masks their Luciferianism in new age paganism and Gaia worship. The Lucifer Trust runs the only chapel at the United Nations and the only statue in the UN building is the pagan god Zeus.

CHRIST MIGHT HAVE BEEN CRUCIFIED YESTERDAY

Christ represented the rule of God. The Pharisees worshipped Lucifer. The question facing mankind hasn't changed. Are we going to serve God or Lucifer?

The Satanists have conditioned us to short circuit at the mention of religion. They have made God seem mysterious, unknowable or non-existent.

Christ said, "God is a Spirit, obey Him in spirit and in truth." (John 4:23,24). God is Absolute Love, Truth, Justice, Goodness and Beauty. If you believe these things are real, whether you accomplish them or not, you believe in God.

Love is the principle of human evolution. God wants to be known by His creation. This requires that we obey and become more like Him. We were made in God's image. "Be ye therefore perfect, even as your father which is in heaven is perfect," (Matthew 5:48).The more we embody spiritual ideals, the more God-like and Real we become. The opposite is also true.

We sacrifice ourselves for what we love. If we love God, we sacrifice ourselves to Him. People ask how to fight the New World Order. Nothing would disturb the Illuminati more than a revival of belief in God. Millions willing to fight and die for God scares the hell out of them. That's why they're uprooting Islam.

We are being prepared in consciousness for slavery or destruction. They are laying the groundwork now with the "war on terror." Once they get Islam under control, they will turn their attention on the West in earnest.

In the meantime, the mass media (movies, music and video games, TV) accustoms us to brutality and violence. There is a repetitive and reductive obsession with sex, nudity, bodily functions and homosexuality.

If our leaders weren't Luciferians, the media and the arts would be preoccupied with issues of truth and falsehood, right and wrong, beauty and ugliness. We would be uplifted and inspired.

Instead, we are degraded distracted and deceived, like people with a terminal disease, like squatters in someone else's universe.

If the lllumnati's real purpose is to eliminate God, it follows we should make God the center of our consciousness. People ask, "What should we do?" Don't look for direction from others. Look to God for direction. The best way to fight the darkness is to shine a light.

This is what the Illuminati fear. In the Protocols of the Elders of Zion the author writes: "There is nothing more dangerous to us than personal initiative; if it has genius behind it, such initiative can do more than can be done by millions of people among whom we have sown discord."

Don't feel oppressed by the world. It hasn't changed just because you are now aware of it.

Devote each new day to fulfilling God's

purpose for you – words and thoughts of Henry Makow, Phd.

What follows are statements from people who believe in Lucifer. It is obvious that these people are deluded, sick in the mind, and controlled by demons. These are the people who control governments and economies. These are the people who foster a one world government, and I suspect are building a platform for the Anti-Christ.

CHAPTER SEVEN

Luciferian Doctrine the Illumiati and the Freemasons:

Lucifer and all his works!

The symbol for Lucifer know as "Nephilim Sigil"

This is the "god of the witches" with his arms "he" points to the sky and to earth which represents the old magical creed what is "That which is above is the same as which is below."

WHAT IS IN A NAME? Confessions of a Luciferian:

"As I have stated in some of my earlier hubs, I was a Satanic Priest that started out belonging to "The Church of Satan" and then branched out into a more collective belief system that included several forms of witchcraft and Shamanism. Eventually I chose to perceive my self as a Luciferian, for it just did not sound as ominous or negative as being a Satanist! However, in Anton's LaVay's Satanic Bible, Lucifer is represented by the east and the element of air and considered one of the "four Crown Princes of Hell."

"If you ask most people who admit to following the so called "Luciferian Doctrine" would tell you point blank that it does not have anything to do with Satan! It seems that Lucifer has become a metaphor for those who think that Christianity is an oppressing religion and Lucifer is the "light barer" who brings light and knowledge to mankind! Well before I take you on the journey to see what this Luciferian Doctrine is all about, we should first study the meaning of the word as was originally created in Latin. As it has been stated in other hubs on the subject of Lucifer, this Latin word derives from lucern which means light and ferre which means to bear- in other words, a light bearer. In fact, some will want you to believe that the word Lucifer is nothing more than a type error, that its placement within the Bible was a mistake that had nothing to do with a fallen angel.

"If this is true then Lucifer has become the most powerful "type error" of all time! For even though the word is only mentioned in the very earliest version of the King James Bible does not mean that the word was not used in many other text and has had a great influence and meaning for many philosophies within the Occult!

"However, to get a grasp on the depth of this subject we must travel back to the very beginning of civilization! To start, I would like to ask an important question for you all to ponder. Why do you think Babylon has been such a big deal within the context of the Bible? Why has it been used in metaphor and reference to evil more often than any other nation within the Bible, right up to Revelation?

"Now if you seriously study the occult as I have for over twenty years of my life, you will see that some of the main sources of influence are Babylon and Egypt. In fact I will dare to say that you can find most of the roots to most of the pagan gods, in these two areas of the world. In my hub The Coming of Nibru I already point out the fact the Sumerians were the instigators of most "magical" beliefs and their ancient text has been a huge influence even in today's Ufology.

"The best way for us to connect the dots and get a complete picture of this mysterious entity which has been called Lucifer, is to start in resent times and then work backwards. To do this, let us all gather into my "time hub" and head back to the year 1966! This is a very important year, for a lot of things were happening at the same time that as strange as it may appear at first, was connected! This was of course during the time of the hippie movement or "free love" This is the same year that LSD and other psychedelics became illegal in the U.S.

"Timothy Leary was in jail and the Vietnam War was ragging. It was also "year one" for the "Age of Satan" or "Anno Satanas" If you prefer Latin. This is when Anton Santon LaVay officially started his church on May first. Anton claimed he was presenting some new concepts but what he was actually doing was reintroducing and repackaging concepts that have its roots in prehistory, or at least far enough back that men have lost track of the detail!

"We can, however track some of the concepts that Mr. LaVay used in the Satanic Bible back to other sources that claim to be a translation of magical text that was said to be associated with an Egyptian mage named Abramelin. Or Abra-Melin, who taught a system of magic to Abraham of Worms who was said to be German Jew who lived from c.1362-c.1458. This is a book that was "translated" by Samuel Liddel MacGregor Mathers to English from German. This book is "The Scared Book of Abramelin the Mage."

"Now, the interesting part about this is in this book that was said to be connected to the Hebrew Cabala and it refers to Lucifer! It is also important to understand that Mr. Mathers was one of the founders of the Golden Dawn. This magical order has become one of the most influential organizations in modern Occultism. Samuel Mathers was one of the main mentors of Aleister Crowley. These two men are said to be the elite of the 20th century Occults and yet they did not have a problem with Lucifer coming from a manuscript that was said to originate from Hebrew! It does seem strange does it not?

"For those who are not familiar with Aleister Crowley, he has been considered over all to be the most authoritative influence of modern Occultism. For not only did he excel in ranks of the Golden Dawn he went on to create his own religion complete with its own age, (The Eon of Horus)! Aleister Crowley had a strong connection with what he saw as Lucifer and Horus. It was while he was in Egypt that he said he was contacted by an entity he would call Aiwass who he claimed "dictated" The Book Of The Law to him. This would be the "god" of his new religion which he would call

Thelema. Besides his extensive involvement in the Occult, he was also a poet who wrote a poem about Lucifer. I have decided to only include part of that poem at the end of part one, for I do want to give Mr. Crowley any more print that is needed to convey my point about his belief in Lucifer as an actual presence.

"However, it will be Aleister who leads us back to the Sumerian culture, the very "cradle of civilization." For as he looked back on his life and his views about this alleged spirit that was said to contact him in Egypt, he made the following statement:

"I am now incline to believe that Aiwass is not only the god once held holy in Sumer (or Sumerian), and mine own Guardian Angel, but also a man as I am, in so far as He uses a human body to make His magical link with Mankind, whom He loves!" Okay, so let us take a peek at these so called gods and how they showed there love for mankind!

"The first thing that jumps out at me when I read the translation of the Sumerian text is that there was a strong belief that humans were the slaves of the gods of this ancient city known as Sumer. These gods that have become known as the Anunnaki were said to have created humans to mine gold! This slave mentality must have found its way into the subconscious of the culture and yet, when the descendants of the Sumerians built Babylon they did not perceive themselves as slaves and instead went about conquering and enslaving every country they could! Was it their way to compensate for the fact that there ancestors were once slaves themselves?

"It is time to turn to the Bible verse that is at the heart of this whole discussion, Isaiah 14: 3-27. For it is important to study all of the verses that relate to this subject and then to understand the context in which they are delivered! For I strongly feel that these verses are not only talking about a king of Babylon, but the spirit behind everything Babylon did and still represents today! To clarify my point, let us first take a look at the purpose behind the book Isaiah.

"Similar to the book of Daniel, Isaiah deals with prophecies that helps illuminate God's plan of salvation and God's Judgment of the wicked. This is why I believe that some of the symbolism in Daniel can be applied to Isaiah's time as well! Isaiah words were not just intended for the children of Israel, but also as a direct message to the Assyrian Empire! The most obvious reason for drawing this conclusion is what is declared by "The Lord of Heavens Armies" starting with verse 22..."I myself, have risen against Babylon! I will destroy its children and its children and its children's children." He (God) promises to make Babylon a desolate place and to "sweep the land with destruction." Now then, if we explore just a bit farther into this, we should take a peak at Daniel and what is said about the "spirit prince" of the king of Persia in Daniel 10:12 This is just one illustration that I feel applies to Isaiah 14: 10 "the spirits of world leaders and mighty kings long dead" seems to me that Isaiah is addressing someone with a bit more power that can be represented by a mortal king!

"After spending much time researching this subject for this article and my past research, from a Occultist point of view leads me to the conclusion that God though his prophet Isaiah, was confronting a spiritual presence. This is the same spirit that God has given the title "the Satan." This is again addressed in Ezekiel 28, for it begins speaking about the Prince of Tyre and yet Ezekiel switches gears in verse 1-19 and begins addressing a spirit which was "the model of perfection full of wisdom and exquisite in beauty." This glorious being was "blameless" until evil was found in him (verse 15).

"Before I continue with this "doctrine" that some claim to be the philosophy of the Freemasons and other "secret" organizations, I would like to share two quotes that sums up what I have been attempting to portray in this commentary. The two quotes are from Ephesians 6: 12 using the NLT study Bible and a passage from Aleister Crowley. I will start with Ephesians then move into Aleister's view of Lucifer. "For we are not fighting against flesh and blood enemies, but against evil rulers and authorities of the unseen world, against mighty powers in this dark world, and against evil spirits in the heavenly places..." This to me is the bottom line, for I see life as war involving two spiritual governments. We, as humans must decide what side we are on!

"Hymn to Lucifer."
His body a bloody-ruby radiant

With noble passion, sun-soiled Lucifer
Swept through the dawn colossal, swift
aslant
On Eden's imbecile perimeter.
He blessed nonentity with every curse
And spiced with sorrow the dull soul of sense
Breathed life into the sterile universe,
With Love and Knowledge drove out
innocence
the key of Joy is disobedience.

"Now the reason why I use this passage from the poem, is the last line which was the mind set I had when I practiced the Occult. In a lot of ways I was rebellious for disobedience sake alone! I have decided that since this subject is so extensive and controversial, that I would break it into "bit size chunks". This first section has taken a peek at the circumstance behind the use of the word Lucifer while the second hub will dive more deeply into the beliefs involved with Lucifer.

"Before I end this article I would like you to consider one more statement which is in fact one of the most profound and conclusive statements to do with occult theory and that is..."That which is above is the same as that which is below" It is this one statement that is said to be behind all magical principals. To me, this brings it back to "the Serpent's "original lie..."You will be like gods knowing both good and evil." Another way to put it would be "all is one and one is all"...which of course is from Led Zeppelin's "Stair-way to heaven."

Core Beliefs:

Unlike the Atheism of many satanic organizations today, we believe that there is more to life than what meets the eye. The following is a brief summary of our beliefs:

1. We believe that the source of all creation (the Plethora) is beyond Mans comprehension and includes all things and nothing.

2. We believe all things are an emanation of the Plethora.

3. We believe that all physical things originate in the spiritual realm and descend to manifest on the physical plane of existence.

4. We believe all things are connected through the Plethora.

5. We believe in the existence of Satan/Lucifer as an actual entity, who was/is another emanation of the Plethora and helps Man to advance spiritually towards AAsar-Un-Nepher (oneself made perfect).

6. We believe Satan/ Lucifer is the real creator of this world, and truly the Lord of this World.

7. We believe YHVH, the blind idiot god, in his thirst for power, usurped Lucifer, and seeks to enslave and destroy all mankind.

8. We believe in the existence of many daemons (or spirits), which help us in our Magic and spiritual advancement.

9. We believe the daemons we work with should be treated with respect. (This means we do not in any way force them to work with us against their will).

10. We believe these daemons are neither "good" nor "evil" but rather hold the seeds of both. Therefore, we see them in various shades of gray.

11. While we do use Magic to better our daily lives, we believe the ultimate aim of Magic is to reach ones own godhood.

12. We believe if necessary, and we so desire, Lucifer may send us back to live many life times to accomplish this goal.

13. We see no distinction between White and Black Magic. Magic is Magic, and we use whatever magical techniques best serve our purpose at the time. Much of our magic is daemonic in nature, seeing how we work with the daemons toward our spiritual advancement.

14. We believe in free thought, as we are all individuals. One must learn to think for oneself, ask questions, do the research, study, ask thy daemon, then decide for yourself.

15. We believe there is no inherent virtue in the morality of society, but because we live in said society, if one chooses to live outside the moral codes of society, they must be ready and willing to take responsibility for their actions.

This is some sick stuff, but I have included it in this book as information as to what the enemy believes. They believe in Lucifer and Lucifer is their power source. And that makes them dangerous!

CHAPTER EIGHT

Luciferianism is a belief system that venerates the essential characteristics that are affixed to Lucifer. The tradition, influenced by Gnosticism, usually reveres Lucifer not as the Devil, but as a rescuer or guiding spirit or even the true god as opposed to Jehovah.

Luciferianism is identified by some people as an auxiliary of Satanism, due to the popular identification of Lucifer with Satan. Some Luciferians accept this identification or consider Lucifer the light bearer aspect of Satan. Others reject it, arguing that Lucifer is a more positive ideal than Satan.

Historical Luciferianism

The Gesta Treverorum records that, in 1231, heretics began to be persecuted throughout Germany. Among them were Luciferians principally in the Archdiocese of

Trier, but also Mainz and Cologne. Over the following three years, several people were burned as a result. According to a papal letter from Gregory IX, Vox in Rama, dated from July 13, 1233, one of the claims made by the Luciferians was that Lucifer had been cast out of Heaven unjustly. Women were implicated in the cult, and the Church accused those named as heretics of sexual perversities. The chronicler of the Gesta seems, however, to have confused Luciferians with the Cathars in some respects.

On the other hand, Richard Cavendish has argued: "The confessions Conrad of Marburg extracted were apparently made without torture, but under the threat of death if the victim did not confess. If these confessions were accurate, the Luciferans were full-blown Satanists. They worshiped the Devil as creator and ruler of the world, complained that he had been unjustly and treacherously banished from Heaven, and believed that he would overthrow the God of the Christians and return to Heaven, when they would enjoy eternal happiness with him. They reveled in whatever displeased the Christian God and hated whatever pleased him.

The following is a portion of the speech that President John F. Kennedy gave at the Waldorf-Astoria Hotel on April 27, 1961. "The President and the Press" before the American Newspaper Publishers Association.

"The very word "secrecy" is repugnant in a free and open society; and we are as a people inherently and historically opposed to secret societies, to secret oaths and secret proceedings. We decided long ago that the dangers of excessive and unwarranted concealment of pertinent facts far outweighed the dangers which are cited to justify it. Even today, there is little value in opposing the threat of a closed society by imitating its arbitrary restrictions. Even today, there is little value in insuring the survival of our nation if our traditions do not survive with it. And there is very grave danger that an announced need for increased security will be seized upon those anxious to expand its meaning to the very limits of official censorship and concealment. That I do not intend to permit to the extent that it is in my control. And no official of my Administration, whether his rank is high or low, civilian or military, should interpret my words here tonight as an excuse to censor the news, to stifle dissent, to cover up our mistakes or to withhold from the press and the public the facts they deserve to know.

"For we are opposed around the world by a monolithic and ruthless conspiracy that relies on covert means for expanding its sphere of influence--on infiltration instead of invasion, on subversion instead of elections, on intimidation instead of free choice, on guerrillas by night instead of armies by day. It is a system which has conscripted vast human and material resources into the building of a tightly knit, highly efficient machine that combines military, diplomatic, intelligence, economic, scientific and political operations.

"Its preparations are concealed, not published. Its mistakes are buried not headlined. Its dissenters are silenced, not praised. No expenditure is questioned, no rumor is printed, no secret is revealed.

"No President should fear public scrutiny of his program. For from that scrutiny comes understanding; and from that understanding comes support or opposition. And both are necessary. I am not asking your newspapers to support the Administration, but I am asking your help in the tremendous task of informing and alerting the American people. For I have complete confidence in the response and dedication of our citizens whenever they are fully informed.

"I not only could not stifle controversy among your readers-- I welcome it. This Administration intends to be candid about its errors; for as a wise man once said: "An error does not become a mistake until you refuse to correct it." We intend to accept full responsibility for our errors; and we expect you to point them out when we miss them.

"Without debate, without criticism, no Administration and no country can succeed-- and no republic can survive. That is why the Athenian lawmaker Solon decreed it a crime for any citizen to shrink from controversy. And that is why our press was protected by the First (emphasized) Amendment-- the only business in America specifically protected by the Constitution-- not primarily to amuse and entertain, not to emphasize the trivial and sentimental, not to simply "give the public what it wants"--but to inform, to arouse, to reflect, to state our dangers and our opportunities, to indicate our crises and our choices, to lead, mold, educate and sometimes even anger public opinion.

"This means greater coverage and analysis of international news-- for it is no longer far away and foreign but close at hand and local. It means greater attention to improved understanding of the news as well as improved transmission. And it means, finally, that government at all levels, must meet its obligation to provide you with the fullest possible information outside the narrowest limits of national security...

"And so it is to the printing press--to the recorder of mans deeds, the keeper of his conscience, the courier of his news-- that we look for strength and assistance, confident that with your help man will be what he was born to be: free and independent."

President Kennedy was assassinated because of his stand against the Illuminati, against his stand of secret societies, against his stand of the Federal Reserve System, and he was not the only president the Illuminati has killed.

Is America a Police State? – Speech by U.S.Congressman Ron Paul:

Below is a truncated version of a speech by congressman Ron Paul expressing his views on governmental encroachment of personal liberties after 9/11.

"My subject today is whether America is a police state. I'm sure the large majority of Americans would answer this in the negative. Most would associate military patrols, martial law and summary executions with a police state, something obviously not present in our everyday activities. However, those with knowledge of Ruby Ridge, Mount Carmel and other such incidents may have a different opinion.

"The principal tool for sustaining a police state, even the most militant, is always economic control and punishment by denying disobedient citizens such things as jobs or places to live, and by levying fines and imprisonment. The military is more often used in the transition phase to a totalitarian state. Maintenance for long periods is usually accomplished through economic controls on commercial transactions, the use of all property, and political dissent. Peaceful control through these efforts can be achieved without storm troopers on our street corners.

"Terror and fear are used to achieve complacency and obedience, especially when citizens are deluded into believing they are still a free people. The changes, they are assured, will be minimal, short-lived, and necessary, such as those that occur in times of a declared war. Under these conditions, most citizens believe that once the war is won, the restrictions on their liberties will be reversed. For the most part, however, after a declared war is over, the return to normalcy is never complete. In an undeclared war, without a precise enemy and therefore no precise ending, returning to normalcy can prove illusory.

"We have just concluded a century of wars, declared and undeclared, while at the same time responding to public outcries for more economic equity. The question, as a result of these policies, is: "Are we already living in a police state?" If we are, what are we going to do about it? If we are not, we need to know if there's any danger that we're moving in that direction.

"Most police states, surprisingly, come about through democratic process with majority support. During a crisis, the rights of individuals and the minority are more easily trampled, which is more likely to condition a nation to become a police state than a military coup. Promised benefits initially seem to exceed the cost in dollars or lost freedom. When people face terrorism or great fear- from whatever source- the tendency to demand economic and physical security over liberty and self-reliance proves irresistible. The masses are easily led to believe that security and liberty are mutually exclusive, and demand for security far exceeds that for liberty.

"Once it's discovered that the desire for both economic and physical security that prompted the sacrifice of liberty inevitably led to the loss of prosperity and no real safety, it's too late. Reversing the trend from authoritarian rule toward a freer society becomes very difficult, takes a long time, and entails much suffering. Although dissolution of the Soviet empire was relatively non-violent at the end, millions suffered from police suppression and economic deprivation in the decades prior to 1989.

"But what about here in the United States? With respect to a police state, where are we and where are we going?

"Let me make a few observations:

"Our government already keeps close tabs on just about everything we do and requires official permission for nearly all of our activities.

"One might take a look at our Capitol for any evidence of a police state. We See: barricades, metal detectors, police, military soldiers at times, dogs, ID badges required for every move, vehicles checked at airports and throughout the Capitol. The people are totally disarmed, except for the police and the criminals. But worse yet, surveillance cameras in Washington are everywhere to ensure our safety.

"The terrorist attacks only provided the cover for the do-gooders who have been planning for a long time before last September to monitor us "for our own good." Cameras are used to spy on our drug habits, on our kids at school, on subway travelers, and on visitors to every government building or park. There's not much evidence of an open society in

Washington, DC, yet most folks do not complain- anything goes if it's for government-provided safety and security.

"If this huge amount of information and technology is placed in the hands of the government to catch the bad guys, one naturally asks, What's the big deal? But it should be a big deal, because it eliminates the enjoyment of privacy that a free society holds dear. The personal information of law-abiding citizens can be used for reasons other than safety- including political reasons. Like gun control, people control hurts law-abiding citizens much more than the law-breakers.

"Social Security numbers are used to monitor our daily activities. The numbers are given at birth, and then are needed when we die and for everything in between. This allows government record keeping of monstrous proportions, and accommodates the thugs who would steal others' identities for criminal purposes. This invasion of privacy has been compounded by the technology now available to those in government who enjoy monitoring and directing the activities of others. Loss of personal privacy was a major problem long before 9/11.

"Centralized control and regulations are required in a police state. Community and individual state regulations are not as threatening as the monolith rules and regulations written by Congress and the federal bureaucracy. Law and order has been federalized in many ways and we are moving inexorably in that direction.

"Almost all of our economic activities depend upon receiving the proper permits from the federal government. Transactions involving guns, food, medicine, smoking, drinking, hiring, firing, wages, politically correct speech, land use, fishing, hunting, buying a house, business mergers and acquisitions, selling stocks and bonds, and farming all require approval and strict regulation from our federal government. If this is not done properly and in a timely fashion, economic penalties and even imprisonment are likely consequences.

"Because government pays for much of our health care, it's conveniently argued that any habits or risk-taking that could harm one's health are the prerogative of the federal government, and are to be regulated by explicit rules to keep medical-care costs down. This same argument is used to require helmets for riding motorcycles and bikes.

"Not only do we need a license to drive, but we also need special belts, bags, buzzers, seats and environmentally dictated speed limits or a policeman will be pulling us over to levy a fine, and he will be toting a gun for sure.

"The states do exactly as they're told by the federal government, because they are threatened with the loss of tax dollars being returned to their state- dollars that should have never been sent to DC in the first place, let alone used to extort obedience to a powerful federal government.

"Over 80,000 federal bureaucrats now carry guns to make us toe the line and to enforce the thousands of laws and tens of thousands of regulations that no one can possibly understand. We don't see the guns, but we all know they're there, and we all know we can't fight "City Hall," especially if it's "Uncle Sam."

"All 18-year-old males must register to be ready for the next undeclared war. If they don't, men with guns will appear and enforce this congressional mandate. "Involuntary servitude" was banned by the 13th Amendment, but courts don't apply this prohibition to the servitude of draftees or those citizens required to follow the dictates of the IRS- especially the employers of the country, who serve as the federal government's chief tax collectors and information gatherers. Fear is the tool used to intimidate most Americans to comply to the tax code by making examples of celebrities. Leona Helmsley and Willie Nelson know how this process works.

"Economic threats against business establishments are notorious. Rules and regulations from the EPA, the ADA, the SEC, the LRB, OSHA, etc. terrorize business owners into submission, and those charged accept their own guilt until they can prove themselves innocent. Of course, it turns out it's much more practical to admit guilt and pay the fine. This serves the interest of the authoritarians because it firmly establishes just who is in charge.

"Information leaked from a government agency like the FDA can make or break a company within minutes. If information is leaked, even inadvertently, a company can be destroyed, and individuals involved in revealing government-monopolized information can be sent to prison. Even though economic crimes are serious offenses in the United States, violent crimes sometimes evoke more sympathy and fewer penalties. Just look at the O.J. Simpson case as an example.

"Efforts to convict Bill Gates and others like him of an economic crime are astounding, considering his contribution to economic progress, while sources used to screen out terrorist elements from our midst are tragically useless. If business people are found guilty of even the suggestion of collusion in the marketplace, huge fines and even imprisonment are likely consequences.

"Price fixing is impossible to achieve in a free market. Under today's laws, talking to, or consulting with, competitors can be easily construed as "price fixing" and involve a serious crime, even with proof that the so-called collusion never generated monopoly-controlled prices or was detrimental to consumers.

"Lawfully circumventing taxes, even sales taxes, can lead to serious problems if a high profile person can be made an example.

"One of the most onerous controls placed on American citizens is the control of speech through politically correct legislation.

"Derogatory remarks or off-color jokes are justification for firings, demotions, and the destruction of political careers. The movement toward designating penalties based on the category to which victims belong, rather the nature of the crime itself, has the thought police patrolling the airways and byways. Establishing relative rights and special penalties for subjective motivation is a dangerous trend.

"All our financial activities are subject to "legal" searches without warrants and without probable cause. Tax collection, drug usage, and possible terrorist activities "justify" the endless accumulation of information on all Americans.

"Government control of medicine has prompted the establishment of the National Medical Data Bank. For efficiency reasons, it is said, the government keeps our medical records for our benefit. This, of course, is done with vague and useless promises that this information will always remain confidential just like all the FBI information in the past!

"Personal privacy, the sine qua non of liberty, no longer exists in the United States. Ruthless and abusive use of all this information accumulated by the government is yet to come. The Patriot Act has given unbelievable power to listen, read, and monitor all our transactions without a search warrant being issued after affirmation of probably cause. "Sneak and peak" and blanket searches are now becoming more frequent every day. What have we allowed to happen to the 4th Amendment?

"It may be true that the average American does not feel intimidated by the encroachment of the police state. I'm sure our citizens are more tolerant of what they see as mere nuisances because they have been deluded into believing all this government supervision is necessary and helpful- and besides they are living quite comfortably, material wise. However the reaction will be different once all this new legislation we're passing comes into full force, and the material comforts that soften our concerns for government regulations are decreased. This attitude then will change dramatically, but the trend toward the authoritarian state will be difficult to reverse.

"What government gives with one hand- as it attempts to provide safety and security- it must, at the same time, take away with two others.

"When the majority recognizes that the monetary cost and the results of our war against terrorism and personal freedoms are a lot less than promised, it may be too late.

"I'm sure all my concerns are unconvincing to the vast majority of Americans, who not only are seeking but also are demanding they be made safe from any possible attack from anybody, ever. I grant you this is a reasonable request.

"The point is, however, there may be a much better way of doing it. We must remember, we don't sit around and worry that some Canadian citizen is about to walk into New York City and set off a nuclear weapon. We must come to understand the real reason is that there's a difference between the Canadians and all our many friends and the Islamic radicals. And believe me, we're not the target because we're "free and prosperous".

"The argument made for more government controls here at home and expansionism overseas to combat terrorism is simple and goes like this: "If we're not made safe from potential terrorists, property and freedom have no meaning." It is argued that first we must have life and physical and economic security, with continued abundance, then we'll talk about freedom.

"It reminds me of the time I was soliciting political support from a voter and was boldly put down: "Ron," she said, "I wish you would lay off this freedom stuff; it's all nonsense. We're looking for a Representative who will know how to bring home the bacon and help our area, and you're not that person." Believe me, I understand that argument; it's just that I don't agree that is what should be motivating us here in the Congress.

"That's not the way it works. Freedom does not preclude security. Making security the highest priority can deny prosperity and still fail to provide the safety we all want.

"The Congress would never agree that we are a police state. Most members, I'm sure, would argue otherwise. But we are all obligated to decide in which direction we are going. If we're moving toward a system that enhances individual liberty and justice for all, my concerns about a police state should be reduced or totally ignored. Yet, if, by chance, we're moving toward more authoritarian control than is good for us, and moving toward a major war of which we should have no part, we should not ignore the dangers. If current policies are permitting a serious challenge to our institutions that allow for our great abundance, we ignore them at great risk for future generations".

CHAPTER NINE

World Depopulation is a Prime Agenda of the Illuminati:

"And I looked, and behold a pale horse: and his name that sat on him was Death, and Hell followed with him. And power was given unto them over the fourth part of the earth, to kill with sword, and with hunger, and with death, and with the beasts of the earth". (Revelation chapter 6)

We are scheduled to be killed by the Illuminati - the power elite who rule governments and economies.

The world population is the sum total of all living humans on Earth. As of today, it is estimated to number 7.029 billion by the United States Census Bureau (USCB). The

USCB estimates that the world population exceeded 7 billion on March 12, 2012. World population is expected to reach 10.5 billion by 2050.

The Illuminati calls the world's people "useless eaters" and they have plans to depopulate the world to their acceptable levels. According to the Georgia Guidestones, the acceptable level is a half billion people. That means 6.5 billion people must die.

The Georgia Guidestones: On one of the highest hilltops in Elbert County, Georgia stands a huge granite monument. Engraved in eight different languages on the four giant stones that support the common capstone are 10 Guides, or commandments. That monument is alternately referred to as The Georgia Guidestones, or the American Stonehenge. Though relatively unknown to most people, it is an important link to the Occult Hierarchy that dominates the world in which we live.

The origin of that strange monument is shrouded in mystery because no one knows the true identity of the man, or men, who commissioned its construction. All that is known for certain is that in June 1979, a well-dressed, articulate stranger visited the office of the Elberton Granite Finishing

Company to build an edifice to transmit a message to mankind. He identified himself as R. C. Christian, but it soon became apparent that was not his real name. He said that he represented a group of men who wanted to offer direction to humanity, but to date, decades later, no one knows who R. C. Christian really was, or the names of those he represented. Several things are apparent. The messages engraved on the Georgia Guidestones deal with four major fields: (1) Governance and the establishment of a world government, (2) Population and reproduction control, (3) The environment and man's relationship to nature, and (4) Spirituality.

THE MESSAGE OF THE GEORGIA GUIDESTONES:

1. Maintain humanity under 500,000,000 in perpetual balance with nature.
2. Guide reproduction wisely - improving fitness and diversity.
3. Unite humanity with a living new language.
4. Rule passion - faith - tradition - and all things with tempered reason.
5. Protect people and nations with fair laws and just courts.

6. Let all nations rule internally resolving external disputes in a world court.

7. Avoid petty laws and useless officials.

8. Balance personal rights with social duties.

9. Prize truth - beauty - love - seeking harmony with the infinite.

10. Be not a cancer on the earth - Leave room for nature - Leave room for nature.

Limiting the population of the earth to 500 million will require the extermination of nine-tenths of the world's people. The American Stonehenge's reference to establishing a world court foreshadows the current move to create an International Criminal Court and a world government. The Guidestones' emphasis on preserving nature anticipates the environmental movement of the 1990s, and the reference to "seeking harmony with the infinite" reflects the current effort to replace Judeo-Christian beliefs with a new spirituality.

The message of the American Stonehenge also foreshadowed the current drive for Sustainable Development. Any time you hear the phrase "Sustainable Development" used, you should substitute the term "socialism" to be able to understand what is intended control of reproduction, world governance, the importance of nature and the environment, and a new spirituality. The similarity between the ideas engraved on the Georgia Guidestones and those espoused in the Earth Charter reflect the common origins of both.

Yoko Ono, the widow of John Lennon, was recently quoted as referring to the American Stonehenge, saying:

"I want people to know about the stones ... We're headed toward a world where we might blow ourselves up and maybe the globe will not exist ... it's a nice time to reaffirm ourselves, knowing all the beautiful things that are in this country and the Georgia Stones symbolize that."

What is the true significance of the American Stonehenge, and why is its covert message important? Because it confirms the fact that there was a covert group intent on:

(1) Dramatically reducing the population of the world.
(2) Promoting environmentalism.

(3) Establishing a world government.
(4) Promoting a new spirituality.

Certainly the group that commissioned the Georgia Guidestones is one of many similar groups working together toward a New World Order, a new world economic system, and a new world spirituality. Behind those groups, however, are dark spiritual forces. Without understanding the nature of those dark forces it is impossible to understand the unfolding of world events.

The fact that most Americans have never heard of the Georgia Guidestones or their message to humanity reflects the degree of control that exists today over what the American people think. We ignore that message at our peril.

The Illuminati Depopulation Agenda

While the global elite construct underground bunkers, eat organic and hoard seeds in Arctic vaults; the global poor are being slowly starved thanks to high commodity prices and poisoned with genetically modified (GMO) food.

Austerity measures aimed largely at the poor are being imposed on all the nations of the world. Weather events grow more deadly and brushfire wars more frequent. An AK-47 can be obtained for $49 in the markets of West Africa. The depopulation campaign of the inbred Illuminati bankers is accelerating.

In 1957 President Dwight Eisenhower, who later warned of a "military-industrial complex", commissioned a panel of scientists to study the issue of overpopulation. The scientists put forth Alternatives I, II and III, advocating both the release of deadly viruses and perpetual warfare as means to decrease world population.

The first supposition dovetailed nicely with the pharmaceutical interests of the Rockefellers. According to Nexus magazine, the Rockefellers own one-half of the US pharmaceutical industry, which would reap billions developing medicines to "battle" the deadly viruses about to be released.

In 1969 the Senate Church Committee discovered that the US Defense Department (DOD) had requested a budget of tens of millions of taxpayer dollars for a program to speed development of new viruses which target and destroy the human immune system.

DOD officials testified before Congress that they planned to produce, "a synthetic biological agent, an agent that does not naturally exist and for which no natural immunity could be acquired...Most important is that it might be refractory to the immunological and therapeutic processes upon which we depend to maintain our relative freedom from infectious disease." House Bill 5090 authorized the funds and MK-NAOMI was carried out at Fort Detrick, Maryland.

Out of this research came the AIDS virus which was targeted at "undesirable elements" of the population. The first AIDS viruses were administered through a massive smallpox vaccine campaign in central and southern Africa by the World Health Organization in 1977. A year later ads appeared in major US newspapers soliciting "promiscuous gay male volunteers" to take part in a Hepatitis B vaccine study.

The program targeted male homosexuals age 20-40 in New York City, Los Angeles, Chicago, St. Louis and San Francisco. It was administered by the US Centers for Disease Control which, under its earlier incarnation as the US Public Health Department in Atlanta, oversaw the Tuskegee syphilis experiments on African American males.

San Francisco has been a target of numerous CIA experiments, due to its high population of left-leaning and gay citizens, which the Illuminati views as "undesirables".

According to Dr. Eva Snead, San Francisco has one of the highest cancer rates in the country. For years Malathion- first developed by the Nazis- was sprayed over the city by helicopters from the CIA's Evergreen Air, whose Arizona base is used, according to author William Cooper, as CIA transshipment point for Columbian cocaine. The mysterious Legionnaire's Disease occurs often in San Francisco and the CIA's MK-ULTRA mind control bad acid program was based there.

The intellectual force behind the introduction of AIDS was the Bilderberger Group, which became fixated on population control after WWII. Author Cooper says the Policy Committee of the Bilderbergers gave orders to DOD to introduce the AIDS virus.

The Bilderbergers are close to the Club of Rome, which was founded on a Rockefeller estate near Bellagio, Italy and is backed by the same European Black Nobility who frequent Bilderberger meetings. A 1968 study by the Club of Rome advocated lowering the birth rate and increasing the death rate. Club founder Dr. Aurelio Peccei made a top-secret recommendation to introduce a microbe that would attack the auto-immune system, then develop a vaccine as a prophylactic for the global elite.

One month after the 1968 Club of Rome meeting Paul Ehrlich published The Population Bomb. The book hints at a draconian depopulation plan in the works. On page seventeen Ehrlich writes, "The problem could have been avoided by population control...so that a 'death rate solution' did not have to occur."

A year later MK-NAOMI was born. Peccei himself authored the Club of Rome's much-touted Global 2000 report, which President Jimmy Carter pushed on his BCCI shakedown cruise of Africa. Peccei wrote in the report, "Man is now vested with unprecedented, tremendous responsibilities and thrown into the role of moderator of life on the planet- including his own".

The Bilderbergers were behind the Haig-Kissinger Depopulation Policy, a driving force at the State Department and administered by the National Security Council. Pressure is applied to Third World countries to reduce their populations.

Those that do not comply see their US aid withheld or are subject to Pink Plan low-intensity war that targets civilians, especially women of child-bearing age. In Africa famine and brush-fire wars are encouraged.

AK-47 rifles can be bought at West African markets for under $50. The same is true in the markets of Peshawar, Pakistan. In 1975, a year after attending a Club of Rome conference on the topic, then Secretary of State Kissinger founded the Office of Population Affairs (OPA).

Latin American OPA case officer Thomas Ferguson spilled the beans on OPA's agenda when he stated, "There is a single theme behind all our work; we must reduce population levels.

"Either they do it our way, through nice clean methods or they will get the kind of mess that we have in El Salvador, or in Iran, or in Beirut...Once population is out of control it requires authoritarian government, even fascism, to reduce it...The professionals aren't interested in reducing population for humanitarian reasons...Civil wars are somewhat drawn-out ways to reduce population. The quickest way to reduce population is through famine like in Africa.

"We go into a country and say, here is your goddamn development plan. Throw it out the window. Start looking at your population...if you don't ...then you'll have an El Salvador or an Iran, or worse, a Cambodia".

Ferguson said of El Salvador, "To accomplish what the State Department deems adequate population control, the civil war (run by CIA) would have to be greatly expanded.

"You have to pull all the males into fighting and kill significant numbers of fertile, child-bearing age females. You are killing a small number of males and not enough fertile females to do the job...If the war went on 30-40 years, you might accomplish something. Unfortunately, we don't have too many instances of this to study".

Report from Iron Mountain

In 1961 Kennedy Administration officials McGeorge Bundy, Robert McNamara and Dean Rusk, all CFR and Bilderberger members, led a study group which looked into "the problem of peace". The group met at Iron Mountain, a huge underground corporate nuclear shelter near Hudson, New York, where CFR think tank The Hudson Institute is located.

The bunker contains redundant offices in case of nuclear attack for Exxon Mobil, Royal Dutch/Shell and JP Morgan Chase. A copy of the group discussions, known as Report from Iron Mountain, was leaked by a participant and published in 1967 by Dial Press.

The report's authors saw war as necessary and desirable stating "War itself is the basic social system, within which other secondary modes of social organization conflict or conspire. (War is) the principal organizing force...the essential economic stabilizer of modern societies."

The group worried that through "ambiguous leadership" the "ruling administrative class" might lose its ability to "rationalize a desired war", leading to the "actual disestablishment of military institutions".

The report goes on to say, "...the war system cannot responsibly be allowed to disappear until...we know exactly what we plan to put in its place...The possibility of war provides the sense of external necessity without which no government can long remain in power...The basic authority of a modern state over its people resides in its war powers. War has served as the last great safeguard against the elimination of necessary classes."

Historian Howard Zinn described this conundrum when he wrote, "American capitalism needed international rivalry- and periodic war- to create an artificial community of interest between rich and poor, supplanting the genuine community of interest among the poor that showed itself in sporadic movements".

The Iron Mountain gang was not the first to discover the virtues of war. In 1909 the trustees of the Andrew Carnegie Foundation for International Peace met to discuss pre-WWI American life. Many of the participants were members of Skull & Bones. They concluded, "There are no known means more efficient than war, assuming the objective is altering the life of an entire people...How do we involve the United States in a war?"

The Report from Iron Mountain goes on to propose a proper role for those of the lower classes, crediting military institutions with providing antisocial elements with an acceptable role in the social structure.

The younger and more dangerous of these hostile social groupings have been kept under control by the Selective Service System...A possible surrogate for the control of potential enemies of society is the reintroduction, in some form consistent with modern technology and political process, of slavery...The development of a sophisticated form of slavery may be an absolute prerequisite for social control in a world at peace.

The Iron Mountain goons, though thrilled by the idea of slavery, listed as other socioeconomic substitutions for war: a comprehensive social welfare program, a giant open-ended space program aimed at unreachable targets, a permanent arms inspection regime, an omnipresent global police and peacekeeping force, massive global environmental pollution which would require a large labor pool to clean up, socially-oriented blood sports and a comprehensive eugenics program.

The Iraqi genocide fulfilled the dreams of the Club of Rome Zero Population Growth maniacs, while also providing a testing ground for two of the war substitutes proposed by the Iron Mountain fascists: an arms inspection regime and UN peacekeepers. Both concepts gained traction in the international community thanks to the Gulf War.

Let the Iraqi Genocide Begin

Estimates of Iraqi casualties during the Gulf War are sobering. Some organizations like Greenpeace put the death toll at near one million people. It was a war in which the media was denied access on a scale never before seen, so casualty figures vary greatly.

According to Tony Murphy, a researcher at the International War Crimes Tribunal, the US attack on Iraq killed 125,000 civilians, while destroying 676 schools, 38 hospitals, 8 major hydroelectric dams, 11 power plants, 119 power substations and half the country's telephone lines. The attacks occurred mostly at night when people were most vulnerable.

In the months following the war the death rate of Iraqi children under five tripled. Thirty-eight percent of these deaths were caused by diarrhea. Victor Filatov, a Russian journalist reporting for Sovetskaya Rossiya from post-war Baghdad wrote, "What further bloodshed do these barbarians of the 20th century need? I thought the Americans had changed since Vietnam...but no, they never change. They remain true to themselves."

According to former US Attorney General Ramsey Clark, the US was found guilty of nineteen war crimes against Iraq before the International War Crimes Tribunal. The US dropped 88,000 tons of bombs on Iraq during the Gulf War and has rained down countless more bombs since.

Many bombs were tipped with armor

piercing depleted uranium (DU) warheads, which may account for chronic Iraqi health problems. Dr. Siegwart-Horst Gunther, a German physician who came to Iraq to help its people, became gravely ill when he handled just one cigar-sized fragment from a DU warhead. Dr. Gunther measured the tiny object's radioactivity to be 11 microSv per hour, whereas an acceptable exposure is no more than 300 microSv per year. Three hundred tons of DU ammunition was deployed during the war.

Many believe DU is responsible for Gulf War Syndrome, which has killed and permanently injured many US soldiers who fought in the Persian Gulf theater. Since 2000, nearly 11,000 US Gulf War veterans have died from Gulf War Syndrome, while the Pentagon continues to cover up this travesty.

CHAPTER TEN

Satanism & Psychotronic Warfare

The US also tested numerous top-secret high-tech weapons systems in the Gulf theatre, while utilizing some old low-frequency favorites. When Iraqi ground forces surrendered, many of them were in a state of delirium and lethargy that could have been induced by extremely low-frequency radio waves, which the US used as a weapon as early as the Vietnam conflict.

Yale University and CIA psychiatrist Dr. Jose Delgado studied mind control for the Company during the 1950's as part of the MK-ULTRA program. Delgado determined, "Physical control of many brain functions is a demonstrated fact...it is even possible to create and follow intentions...By electronic stimulation of specific cerebral structures, movements can be induced by radio command...by remote control."

According to a military document written by Colonel Paul Valley and Major Michael Aquino titled From PSYOP to Mindwar: The Psychology of Victory, the US Army used an operational weapons system "to map the minds of neutral and enemy individuals and then to change them in accordance with US national interests".

The technique was used to secure the surrender of 29,276 armed Viet Cong and North Vietnamese Army soldiers in 1967 and 1968. The US Navy was also heavily involved in "psychotronic" research. Many US soldiers who served near the DMZ that divided North and South Vietnam claimed to see UFOs on a regular basis. The Pentagon Papers revealed that an electronic barrier was placed along the DMZ by the secretive JASON Society.

Major Michael Aquino was an Army psyops specialist in Vietnam, where his unit specialized in drug-inducement, brainwashing, virus injection, brain implants, hypnosis, and use of electromagnetic fields and extremely low-frequency radio waves. After Vietnam, Aquino moved to San Francisco and founded the Temple of Set.

Set is the ancient Egyptian name for

Lucifer. Aquino was now a senior US Military Intelligence official. He'd been given a Top Secret security clearance on June, 9, 1981. Less than a month later an Army intelligence memo revealed that Aquino's Temple of Set was an off-shoot of Anton LaVey's Church of Satan, also headquartered in San Francisco. Two other Set members were Willie Browning and Dennis Mann. Both were Army Intelligence officers.

The Temple of Set was obsessed with military matters and political fascism. It was especially preoccupied with the Nazi Order of the Trapezoid. Aquino's "official" job was history professor at Golden Gate College. The Temple recruited the same Hells Angels who Billy Mellon Hitchcock had used to dole out his bad CIA acid.

Its members frequented prostitutes where they engaged in all manner of sadomasochistic activities. Director of Army Counter-Intelligence Donald Press revealed that Dennis Mann was assigned to the 306 PSYOPS Battalion and that Aquino was assigned to a top secret program known as Presidio.

Presidio was also the name of a

spooky US Army base in what is now the Golden Gate National Recreation Area, which Mikhail Gorbachev reportedly frequented as the Soviet Union was falling apart.

Was Aquino part of an operation to "map the mind" of the Soviet Union's last leader and induce him into proposing both glasnost and perestroika, the two free market policies that ultimately led to the Soviet Union's demise? Remember the curious mark which suddenly appeared on Gorbachev's forehead? Was he implanted with some sort of microchip mind-control device to make him think "in accordance with US national interests"?

Such Orwellian technology is marketed on a regular basis throughout the world. International Healthline Corporation and others sell microchip implants in the US, Russia and Europe. The Humane Society has adopted a policy of micro-chipping all stray pets. The State of Hawaii requires that all pets be micro-chipped.

Six thousand people in Sweden have accepted a microchip in their hand, which they use for all purchases. Trials are also underway in Japan. In July 2002, National

Public Radio reported a similar trial beginning in Seattle. Later in 2002, after a rash of suspicious abductions of young girls, BBC reported that a British company plans to implant children with microchips so that their parents can monitor their whereabouts.

Dr. Carl Sanders, a highly acclaimed electronics engineer, revealed that a microchip project he launched to help people with severed spinal cords was taken over by the Bill Colby's Operation Phoenix in a series of meetings organized by Henry Kissinger.

Sanders says the optimal spot for a microchip implant is just below the hairline on a person's forehead, since the device can be recharged by changes in body temperatures, which are most pronounced there. Interestingly, this is the location of the pineal gland or Third Eye.

The 1986 Emigration Control Act grants the President the power to mandate any kind of ID he deems necessary. Researchers at Southern California have developed a chip which mimics the hippocampus, the part of the brain that deals with memory. Pentagon officials are interested in using it in experiments to create a "super-soldier". Another microchip called Braingate is being implanted in paralyzed people. It allows them to control their environment by simply thinking.

In Iraq, psychological warfare gave way to slow genocide. According to UNICEF, as of late 2001, 1.5 million Iraqi children had died as a result of sanctions, while one child in ten died before their first birthday.

Thalassemia, anemia and diarrhea were the biggest killers and could have been prevented were it not for a chronic shortage of blood and medicine in Iraq due to the sanctions. UN Committee 661 served as arbiter of what constituted a "dual use" item and therefore banned for import into Iraq. As of 2001, over 1,600 Iraqi contracts with Western companies for medical equipment had been blocked by 661.

The Gulf War decimated Iraq's sewer and water treatment systems. Iraqis were forced to drink polluted water, leading to numerous health problems. Iraq was not allowed to import chlorine to clean the water since 661 deemed it a potential chemical weapon.

Electrical power was rationed in three-hour daily increments per household since the Iraqi government couldn't get the parts it needed to fix its power plants after the US bombed its entire power grid. With the devaluation of the Iraqi dinar and the ban on the export of 2.4 million barrels of oil per day, the average Iraqi lived on $2.50 a month-enough to buy a pair of shoes. The only Iraqis not affected were the wealthy elite, who had long ago stashed their savings overseas in US dollars.

UNICEF estimates that 28% of Iraqi children no longer went to school. Before the war almost all children attended. Often families could only afford to send one child to school because of the cost of simple things like backpacks, shoes and notebooks.

Rafah Salam Aziz, Director of Mansour Children's Hospital, said parents were often forced to make similar decisions about their children's lives. Aziz said, "Many times it's easier for a family to let a baby die rather than let the whole family go hungry and get sick."

In 1996 Clinton Defense Secretary William Perry announced a new military buildup in the Persian Gulf. Soon cruise missiles were again raining down on Baghdad. Many nations now grew weary of both US bombing and the sanctions regime, which was brutalizing the Iraqi people while strengthening the grip of Saddam Hussein.

Russian President Boris Yeltsin, whose country signed a deal with Iraq to rebuild its shattered oil sector, said he was disturbed at the use of "extreme and radical force against the Arab world". The Russian opposition offered a more scalding appraisal. Alexander Lebed stating angrily, "The US is like a strong master who spits on everybody."

Turkey, Jordan and Syria all expressed unease over the new round of bombing. Even the Saudis, where Islamic fundamentalism was on the rise and two major bombings had occurred at US bases, now refused to allow the US to use its bases to bomb Iraq. Many countries, including France, began openly flaunting the UN embargo against Iraq in the late 1990's.

Dennis Halliday, former Assistant Secretary of the UN who initially headed the UN Humanitarian Program to Iraq, resigned his post in protest. He said sanctions were demolishing the very class of Iraqi people who wanted to create a better government in the country. He was scornful of the UN Oil for Food Program under which the US received 70% of Iraqi oil. Halliday stated plainly, "We are guilty of committing genocide, through the Security Council, against Iraq."

Halliday's 1998 successor was Hans Van Sponeck, who watched as the UN unfurled the UNSCOM arms inspection regime, paid for by Iraqi oil sales. US inspector Scott Ritter confirmed Iraqi suspicions that UNSCOM was gathering intelligence for CIA and Mossad.

UNSCOM was just the latest CIA tool. In 1996 the Iraqi government claimed international relief agencies, including the World Food Program, which claimed to be helping the Kurds, were actually CIA operatives attempting to destabilize the country.

In fact the CIA had spent more than $20 million in its support of the Iraqi National Congress, led by long-time CIA surrogate Jalal Talibani's PKK Kurdish faction. In January 1997 Iraq uncovered two Mossad spy rings in one month following the attempted assassination of Saddam Hussein's son. Hans Van Sponeck had seen enough. He too resigned in protest.

In early 1999 it was revealed that the US had used UNSCOM to plant electronic bugging devices in the Iraqi Ministry of Defense. Arms inspector Scott Ritter said the CIA was using UNSCOM to "provoke a crisis".

In December 1998 UNSCOM, faced with the embarrassing accusations of espionage, pulled out of Iraq. On December 15th the US launched a new round of bombing. Ritter says intelligence gathered by UNSCOM was used for targeting. UNSCOM spokesman David Kay resurfaced in 2003 calling for a US invasion of Iraq. He now worked for SAIC, which landed numerous Pentagon contracts to rebuild Iraq – Dean Henderson.

The following information speaks for itself:

More Evidence HIV Was Made At Ft. Detrick

From Alan Cantwell MD

I am a physician and AIDS researcher who has authored two books on the man-made origin of HIV/AIDS ("AIDS & THE DOCTORS OF DEATH: AN INQUIRY INTO THE ORIGIN OF THE AIDS EPIDEMIC" and "QUEER BLOOD: THE SECRET AIDS GENOCIDE PLOT.").

On the eve of May 31, 2007, I was sent the most explosive email I have ever received concerning possible insider evidence pertaining to the man-made epidemic of AIDS. The communication was sent by Sue Arrigo, M.D., who claimed she was a physician licensed in California (G50197). Because her email (attached below) was so mind-blowing, I immediately googled Arrigo and found several entries including a note on one website in which Arrigo claimed to have been kidnapped, raped and threatened with death in 2004 (this was NOT mentioned in her email to me). In addition, I checked online and verified that she was indeed a licensed CA physician, although her license expired in December, 2006, and her current residence is in Canada.

In her email Dr. Arrigo asked if I would help her get the word out to interested persons. I would ask that anyone who receives this communication to do all they can to spread the word regarding her accusations that AIDS is a man-made disease.

Over the past two decades there have been only a handful of other physicians and health professionals who have had the courage to alert the public to evidence that AIDS is man-made (namely Robert Strecker MD, William Campbell Douglass MD, Eva Snead MD, and Leonard G Horowitz DDS). In general, their research (books, videos, internet communications) have been ignored by the CDC, the NIH, the AIDS establishment, the major media, etc. -- and merely passed over as "conspiracy theory" and "paranoia." Dr. Arrigo has a long association with the CIA as an expert on biological warfare, and also has apparent ties to the highest powers (and presidents) in the U.S. government. Thus, her insider status makes her an extremely valuable witness to the truth about AIDS and its man-made origin.

Please do all you can to confirm or deny the truth of Dr. Arrigo's accusations -- and to publicize her plight -- and to air her plea on behalf of the abominations of secret biological warfare experimentation and use against human beings.

I have attached the google references to "sue arrigo", her email to me in it's entirety, proof of her CA medical credentials, and a website note of her rape and torture.

In truth and justice,

Alan Cantwell M.D.
alancantwell@sbcglobal.net

On May 31, 2007, at 8:32 PM, Sue Arrigo wrote:

Dear Dr. Cantwell,

Thank you for your courage and integrity in speaking the truth.

As an ex- CIA physician with high level access, I wrote a report for DCI Webster in about 1991 arguing for closure of all the US Bio-Warfare Labs. I did that after reviewing the Ft. Detrick and the CIA's Langley Bio-Warfare Labs's research, looking at their own documents. That review was authorized because Bush, Sr. had sold dangerous Bio-Warfare agents to Hussein, which I ended up having to recover from Iraq. Webster, as a former judge, willing to evaluate the evidence, allowed me to research the field and write a report for him of close to 100 pages and 1000 pages of supporting documents.

Although the focus of my report was why the Bio-Warfare Labs should be closed, the issue of the HIV virus developed by the Ft. Detrick lab formed about 18 pages of my report. At the time I wrote that report, the vaccine for HIV that had been developed in 6 months of work, had already been used by the Cabal since 1983.

It was a crime against humanity that the virus was unleashed on the world, and it continues to be a crime that the vaccine has been kept secret and for private use only. Meanwhile, the outer research to get to a vaccine is an exercise in how not to arrive at a solution before millions more die. The initial "hopes" for HIV per its designers was to be able to walk into Africa and take the resources from a ghost continent. They had hyped it as killing everyone there within a year, in their pre-release reports.

The research at the Labs addressed the fastest way to make vaccines to Bio-warfare agents, both in labs, at a front, and impromptu on a battlefield. That was a pressing concern and one that was researched using millions and millions of dollars.

Briefly, the consensus at the time was that:

1) Any agent from a sick soldier left in a Waring Blender for 8 hours would be broken down well enough to not be infective in small doses (ie. less than a 100 germs). The Labs had made an IgM set of antibodies to sediment out the human HLA antigens by centrifuging it. That allowed the supernatant to be used as a vaccine with little serum sickness problems. A physician in a war zone equipped with a Waring Blender, a blood specimen centrifuge, and a vial of the IgM could make a fast "fresh" vaccine and start inoculating soldiers. The labs tested that using a variety of agents and common cold agents. It was only if one wanted to store the vaccine in vials that one got into the problem of denaturing the proteins of the agent due to heat, chemicals, etc. That was where most of the problems of loss of effectiveness crop up.

2) The Labs found that causing a 1cm by 1cm abrasion until one got lymph and applying a drop of the "fresh vaccine" and a band aid, worked almost as well as an injection. The abrasion could be caused by three fast firm strokes of very fine sand paper over a template with a square of skin bulging through it. This method had much less serum sickness problem. The major problem was occasion keloid and scar formation and superficial infections.

3) The Labs also showed that it was possible to make a crude live vaccine as an emergency directly on the battlefield. The principle was that infection occurs when the body's defenses are overwhelmed but that the body can usually fend off 10 to 50 organisms even of Bio-warfare agents. It was a simple dilution to get the agent into the right ballpark, starting with a secretion of a sick person. Then a drop of that dilute live agent would be placed on an abrasion. That was also tested during war games with colds etc. The diluted material can't be stored for longer than an hour due to the risk of multiplying the agent. It was assumed that in the field it would not be known whether the agent was a virus or a bacteria. A bacteria that divided

every 20 minutes could be 8 fold in quantity after an hour and risk causing the infection one was attempting to prevent. Of course, such a live agent could be extremely dangerous and except in an extreme emergency would not be used.

4) The issue of how to quickly sterilize a make-shift vaccine was also addressed in the research. The best method was to dry the agent, if time permitted. Second best was to preserve the agent in Vodka (40%), not gin, etc., and then to dilute it down to less than 2% alcohol before applying it to the abrasion.

That means that a simple vaccine for HIV can be made by virtually anyone in the world in a short period of time, though it would likely need to be repeated periodically to get and keep the titers up. But repeating it is a good idea anyway as that helps address the mutation problem. So, suppose one took 1 cc of secretions from each of 10 HIV patients in an area (without fungal infections preferably) and mixed them together to have a range of HIV agents. Then one could add 250 cc of Vodka and let it sit a week. Then one could remove a cc of that and add 20 cc of clean water to get a less than 2% alcohol solution. A drop of that could be applied to an abrasion. That, I believe, would give you about 60% protection. Repeating that at intervals of about 2 weeks to a month for 6 months and using new HIV secretions every 6 to 12 months, I think would give one fairly good protection in a person with a normal immune system to start with. Of course, that is a crude method and should be tested for efficacy etc. But it is simple enough to test on sex workers, if they were willing to volunteer. They are at such high risk that the likely benefits almost certainly outweigh the risks. The chief risk would still be sensitization with human HLA proteins. The beauty of using abrasions is that one can wash the vaccine off as soon as any untoward reaction is noticed.

If you know of people doing HIV research who are not controlled by the US Govt, could you please pass this information on to them?

It would be good to get it out to those who could investigate this information with the intention of saving lives with it. Bio- warfare research is immoral and illegal. Unfortunately the US Govt. is accelerating that research and production of secret private vaccines.

Sincerely, Sue Arrigo, MD

(the below is from:
http://www.alternet.org/rights/27771/)

An American Already Tortured By Cheney's Team in the US

Posted by: kunzangwangmo on Nov 11, 2005 10:16 PM

As a coerced CIA asset, I was asked by Cheney in Aug. 2004 to frame Iran as developing nuclear weapons. Because Cheney was afraid of CIA leaks, he gave me the assignment at a Chinese restaurant in DC after hours. It was not the first meeting that I have ever had privately with him as I acted as a negotiator between him and Tenet. Within the CIA I had been an outspoken critic of US wars of aggression, its nuclear first strike plans, and its breaking of nuclear arms control treaties. I spent most of my life as an operative risking my life as a remote viewing spy monitoring and recovering lost WMD.

I am a doctor and the assignment Cheney gave me was to go to Iran as a physician. Once in Iran, a camera crew would be filming when an Iranian agent would rush in to say that he knew a secret bunker where the Iranian govt. was developing nuclear weapons. Cheney admitted that the rest of the filming would occur in Hollywood with a mock up of said lab. Clearly, this was an immoral assignment. There was no way that I was going to have the blood of innocent Iranian women and children on my hands, so I refused. When I did so, Cheney threatened the life of my mother. Since my mother had recently told me she would rather die than have me be emotionally blackmailed in this way, I held to my no.

During the course of our about 40 minute talk, one of his secret service officers interrupted us twice. The next week when I was kidnapped in Virginia, raped and tortured for 4 days, I recognized the voice of that officer as one of the rapists.

It is an outrage that Cheney is advocating torture. He has already shown by his actions, that he will stop at nothing, not even the torture of American born CIA personnel in order to get his way. He has a clear conflict of interest in making money off these wars. Are we, as Americans, going to torture people just so that corrupt officials can line their pockets with oil and war profiteering revenues?

Please write your congresspersons to prevent others being tortured as I was. Cheney and Bush should be impeached for lying to force us into war. We are not winning the war on terrorism, torture is terrorism as anyone who had been through it knows. I was raped and subjected to three mock executions, when will this US reign of terror end?

Sincerely,

Sue Arrigo, MD

CHAPTER ELEVEN

Fort Detrick is a U.S. Army Medical Command installation located in Frederick, Maryland, USA. Historically, Fort Detrick was the center for the United States' biological weapons program (1943–69).

Today, Fort Detrick's 1,200-acre (490 ha) campus supports a multi-governmental community that conducts biomedical research and development, medical materiel management, global medical communications and the study of foreign plant pathogens. It is home to the U.S. Army Medical Research and Materiel Command (USAMRMC), with its bio-defense agency, the U.S. Army Medical Research Institute of Infectious Diseases (USAMRIID). It also hosts the National Cancer Institute-Frederick (NCI-Frederick) and will be home to the National Interagency Confederation for Biological Research (NICBR).

History:

Five farms originally constituted what is today known as "Area A" with 800 acres (320 ha), or the main post area of Fort Detrick, where most installation activities are located. ("Area B" — known as "The Farm" and consisting of nearly 400 acres (160 ha) — was purchased in 1946 to provide a test area west of Rosemont Avenue, then called Yellow Springs Pike. In addition, the post's water and waste water treatment plants comprise about 16 acres (6.5 ha) on the banks of the Monocacy River.)

Detrick Field (1931-43)

Fort Detrick traces its roots to a small municipal airport established at Frederick, Maryland in 1929. It was operated by a single person and the field was one of a string of emergency airfields between Cleveland, Ohio, and Washington, DC until 1938. The field was named in honor of squadron flight surgeon Major Frederick L. Detrick who served in France during World War I and died in June 1931 of a heart attack. The first military presence there was the encampment, on 10 August 1931 (two months after the Major's death), of his unit: the 104th Observation

Squadron of the 29th Division, Maryland National Guard. The Squadron flew de Havilland observation biplanes and Curtiss JN-4 "Jennies".

A concrete and tarmac airfield replaced the grass field in 1939, and an upgraded Detrick Field served as a Cadet Pilot Training Center until the country's entry into World War II. Detrick Field was formally leased from the City of Frederick in 1940 (having previously been leased from the state for just 2 weeks per year). The last airplanes departed Detrick Field in December 1941 and January 1942 after the Japanese attack on Pearl Harbor. All aircraft and pilots in the 104th and the cadet program were reassigned after the Declaration of War to conduct antisubmarine patrols off the Atlantic Coast. The 2nd Bombardment Squadron, U.S. Army Air Corps was reconstituted at Detrick Field between March and September 1942, when it deployed to England to become the nucleus of the new Eighth Air Force headquarters. Thereafter, the base ceased to be an aviation center.

Camp Detrick (1943-56)

On 9 March 1943, the government

purchased 154 acres (62 ha) encompassing the original 92 acres (37 ha) and re-christened the facility "Camp Detrick". The same year saw the establishment of the U.S. Army Biological Warfare Laboratories (USBWL), responsible for pioneering research into biocontainment, decontamination, gaseous sterilization, and agent purification. The first commander, Lt. Col. William S. Bacon, and his successor, Col. Martin B. Chittick, oversaw the initial $1.25 million renovation and construction of the base.

World War II and BW research (1943-45)
Main article: United States biological weapons program

During World War II, Camp Detrick and the USBWL became the site of intensive biological warfare (BW) research using various pathogens. This research was originally overseen by pharmaceuticals executive George W. Merck and for many years was conducted by Ira L. Baldwin, professor of bacteriology at the University of Wisconsin. Baldwin became the first scientific director of the labs. He chose Detrick Field for the site of this exhaustive research effort because of its balance between remoteness of location and proximity to Washington, DC —

as well as to Edgewood Arsenal, the focal point of U.S. chemical warfare research. Buildings and other facilities left from the old airfield — including the large hangar — provided the nucleus of support needed for the startup. The 92 acres (37 ha) of Detrick Field were also surrounded by extensive farmlands that could be procured if and when the BW effort was expanded.

The Army's Chemical Warfare Service was given responsibility and oversight for the effort that one officer described as "cloaked in the deepest wartime secrecy, matched only by ... the Manhattan Project for developing the Atomic Bomb". Three months after the start of construction, an additional $3 million was provided for five additional laboratories and a pilot plant. Lt. Col. Bacon was authorized 85 officers, 373 enlisted personnel, and 80 enlisted Women's Army Auxiliary Corps (WAAC) members under two WAAC officers. At its peak strength in 1945, Camp Detrick had 240 officers and 1,530 enlisted personnel including WAACs.

Post-war years (1946-55)

The elaborate security precautions taken at Camp Detrick were so effective that it was not until January 1946, 4 months after VJ Day that the public learned of the war-time research in biological weapons.

In 1952, the Army purchased over 500 acres (200 ha) more of land located between West 7th Street and Oppossum town Pike to expand the permanent research and development facilities.

Two workers at the base died from exposure to anthrax in the 1950s. Another died in 1964 from viral encephalitis.

There was a building on the base, Building 470 locally referred to as "Anthrax Tower". Building 470 was a pilot plant for testing optimal fermentor and bacterial purification technologies. The information gained in this pilot plant shaped the fermentor technology that was ultimately used by the pharmaceutical industry to revolutionize production of antibiotics and other drugs. Building 470 was torn down in 2003 without any adverse effects on the demolition workers or the environment. The facility acquired the nickname "Fort Doom" while offensive biological warfare research was undertaken there. 5,000 bombs containing anthrax spores were produced at the base during World War II.

From 1945 to 1955 under Project Paperclip and its successors, the U.S. government recruited over 1,600 German and Austrian scientists and engineers in a variety of fields such as aircraft design, missile technology and biological warfare. Among the specialists in the latter field who ended up working in the U.S. were Walter Schreiber, Erich Traub and Kurt Blome, who had been involved with medical experiments on concentration camp inmates to test biological warfare agents. Since Britain, France and the Soviet Union were also engaged in recruiting these scientists, the Joint Intelligence Objectives Agency (JIOA) wished to deny their services to other powers, and therefore altered or concealed the records of their Nazi past and involvement in war crimes.

Testing performed on SDAs

The U.S. General Accounting Office issued a report on September 28, 1994, which stated that between 1940 and 1974, DOD and other national security agencies studied hundreds of thousands of human subjects in tests and experiments involving hazardous substances.

The quote from the study:

Many experiments that tested various biological agents on human subjects, referred to as Operation Whitecoat, were carried out at Fort Detrick, Maryland, in the 1950s. The human subjects originally consisted of volunteer enlisted men. However, after the enlisted men staged a sitdown strike to obtain more information about the dangers of the biological tests, Seventh-day Adventists [SDAs] who were conscientious objectors were recruited for the studies.

The Army purchased an additional 147 acres in 1946 to increase the size of the original "Area A" as well as 398 acres located west of Area A, but not contiguous to it, to provide a test area known as Area B. In 1952, another 502.76 acres were purchased between West 7th Street and Oppossum town Pike to expand the permanent research and development facilities.

Jeffrey Alan Lockwood finds that the biological warfare program at Ft. Detrick began to research the use of insects as disease vectors going back to World War II and also employed German and Japanese scientists after the war who had experimented on human subjects among POWs and concentration camp inmates. Scientists used or attempted to use a wide variety of insects in their biowar plans, including fleas, ticks, ants, lice and mosquitoes—especially mosquitoes that carried the yellow fever virus. They also tested these in the United States. Lockwood thinks that it is very likely that the U.S. did use insects dropped from aircraft during the Korean War to spread diseases, and that the Chinese and North Koreans were not simply engaged in a propaganda campaign when they made these allegations, since the Joint Chiefs of Staff and Secretary of Defense had approved their use in the fall of 1950 at the "earliest practicable time". At that time, it had five bio warfare agents ready for use, three of which were spread by insect vectors. By 1952, the U.S. had dropped insects carrying a wide variety of diseases over China and North Korea, including plague, anthrax, encephalitis, cholera, dysentery, neurotropic viruses, and plant and livestock pathogens.

Fort Detrick (1956-Present)

Cold War years (1956-89)

Camp Detrick was designated a permanent installation for peacetime biological research and development shortly after World War II, but that status was not confirmed until 1956, when the post became Fort Detrick. Its mandate was to continue its previous mission of biomedical research and its role as the world's leading research campus for biological agents requiring specialty containment.

The most recent land acquisition for the Fort was a parcel of less than 3 acres along the Rosemont Avenue fence in 1962, completing the present 1,200 acres.

On Veterans Day, November 11, 1969, President Richard M. Nixon asked the Senate to ratify the 1925 Geneva Protocol prohibiting the use of chemical and biological weapons. Nixon assured Fort Detrick its research would continue. On November 25, 1969, Nixon made a statement outlawing offensive biological research in the United States. Since that time any research done at Fort Detrick has been purely defensive in nature focusing on diagnostics, preventives and treatments for BW infections. This research is undertaken by the U.S. Army Medical Research Institute of Infectious Diseases (USAMRIID) which transitioned from the previous U.S. Army Medical Unit (USAMU) and was renamed in

1969.

Many former laboratories and some land made available by the disestablishment of the offensive biological warfare program were ultimately transferred to the U.S Department of Health and Human Services during the 1970s and later. The National Cancer Research and Development Center (now the National Cancer Institute-Frederick) was established in 1971 on a 69-acre parcel in Area A ceded by the installation.

In 1989 base researchers identified the Ebola virus in a monkey imported to the area from the Philippines.

Post-Cold War (1990-present)

In 2009, author H. P. Albarelli published the book A Terrible Mistake: The Murder of Frank Olson and the CIA's Secret Cold War Experiments about Frank Olson's death and the experiments conducted at Fort Detrick. The book is based on documents released under FOIA and numerous other documents and interviews to the police and investigators, along with a lot of speculation and guessing.

In the 1980s and '90s Jakob Segal made

a claim that Fort Detrick was the site where the United States government "invented" HIV.

USAMRIID had been the principal consultant to the FBI on scientific aspects of the 2001 Anthrax Attacks, which had infected 22 people and killed five. While assisting with the science from the beginning, it also soon became the focus of the FBI's investigation of possible perpetrators. In July 2008, a top U.S. biodefense researcher at USAMRIID committed suicide just as the FBI was about to lay charges relating to the incidents. The scientist, Bruce Edwards Ivins, who had worked for 18 years at USAMRIID, had been told about the impending prosecution. The FBI's identification of Ivins in August 2008 as the Anthrax Attack perpetrator remains controversial and several independent government investigations which will address his culpability are ongoing. Although the anthrax preparations used in the attacks were of different grades, all of the material derived from the same bacterial strain. Known as the Ames strain, it was first researched at USAMRIID. The Ames strain was subsequently distributed to at least fifteen bio-research labs within the U.S. and six locations overseas.

In June, 2008 the Environmental Protection Agency said it planned to add the base to the Superfund list of the most polluted places in the country. On 9 April 2009, "Fort Detrick Area B Ground Water" was added to the list which currently includes 18 other sites within Maryland.

About 7,900 people work at Fort Detrick. The base is the largest employer in Frederick County and contributes more than $500 million into the local economy annually.

In 2012 the United States National Research Council published a report that reviewed two investigations of potential health hazards at Fort Detrick: a 2009 public health assessment conducted by the Agency for Toxic Substances and Disease Registry and a cancer investigation in Frederick County by the Maryland Department of Health and Mental Hygiene and the Frederick County Health Department. The report found the two studies are unable to demonstrate whether people were harmed by groundwater contaminated with toxic pollutants from Area B of Fort Detrick. Furthermore, it is unlikely that additional studies could establish a link, because data on early exposures were not collected and cannot be obtained or reliably estimated now.

Tenant units and organizations

Each branch of the U.S. military is represented among Fort Detrick's 7,800 military, federal and contractor employees. Four cabinet level agencies are represented by activities on the garrison: The U.S. Department of Homeland Security, the U.S. Department of Agriculture, the U.S. Department of Health and Human Services, and the U.S. Department of Defense. The offices and laboratories include the Agriculture Department's Foreign Disease and Weed Science Research Institute, the National Cancer Institute, the Naval Medical Logistics Command and the Telemedicine and Advanced Technology Research Center. Currently under construction is a biotechnology campus that will house civilian and military research centers including units of the Centers for Disease Control and Prevention (CDC), the National Institute of Allergy and Infectious Diseases (NIAID), as well as USAMRIID.

This base and the creation of biological weapons should have been closed years ago, but if it was closed down the government would only open another one – probably underground.

CHAPTER TWELVE

DEEP UNDERGROUND MILITARY BASES
IN AMERICA

The information in this book, like all information, is meant to stir thought about what is going on in our world. I do not personally agree with all of the ideas mentioned here while I do think they are worth considering to better understand what goes on behind the scenes.

Human abduction, mind control facility in the U.K – Project Mannequin

There arc several foreign forces currently holed up in various underground bases. Many of these have been programmed via mind-control techniques. Those have been given 'lists' containing names of citizens that they will be responsible for rounding up.

Red List – These people are the enemies

of the NWO. They are the leaders of patriot groups, outspoken ministers, outspoken talk show hosts, community leaders, and even probably NET leaders. These people will be dragged out of their homes at 4:00 am and will be taken to FEMA detention centers and killed. This will take place approximately 2 weeks before martial law is enforced.

Blue List – these are also enemies of the NWO, but are followers of the Red List folks. These people will be rounded up after martial law is in place, and will be taken to the detention centers and re-educated. Various mind-control techniques will used on them. Most will not survive this. Mr. Springmeier was not specific on exactly who was on the Blue List, but I would guess that people such as you and I are on that list.

Yellow List – these are citizens who know nothing about the NWO and don't want to know. They are considered to be no threat at all and will be instructed as to how to behave and will most likely do whatever they are told. Unfortunately there are too many of these to be effectively controlled, so many will be killed or starved.

Unknown to most Americans is a dark secret, and it's right under our noses. It's the reality of the existence of DEEP UNDERGROUND MILITARY BASES. These Underground bases get prominent play in dark rumors circulating about captured extraterrestrials and alien technology.

The fringe culture rumors of underground alien-human shenanigans are in reality fed by leaks from questionable individuals, usually with intelligence connections. They are simply a ploy utility for the status quo. The whole captured-alien-hardware story is just a highly elaborate hoax to discredit those exposing the reality of these bases.

They are also a cover for the wholesale looting of the federal treasury by the corrupt and cynical secret government.

After Hurricane Katrina left the gulf coast region totally devastated, there were many witnesses coming forward with reports of UNMNTF and UNISF Troops working alongside the Army of the Republic of Mexico Soldiers in the New Orleans area.

When the day of Martial Law comes in

America, the UNISF and UNMNTF troops located in Central America, in the US, and Canada will be deployed to help round up the millions of Americans whose names appear on the CIA Red List and the CIA Blue List.

These troops are Chinese, Russian, German, Polish, Japanese, Ukrainian, Saudi Arabian, Pakistani, Mexican, Honduran, Salvadorean and Chilean, and many are stationed in the deep underground military bases.

When that day comes in America, do not expect the Fox News Network, NBC, CBS, ABC, CNN, BBC News 24 or Reuters to give a full or accurate account of the truth. Mass detentions in camps and the underground bases, along with mass executions will occur, like they have in many other countries like Cambodia, Russia, China, Germany, Poland, Armenia, Georgia, Belorussia, Hungary and the Ukraine over the past 100 years. The best option for many Americans will be to have a safe place in a remote area where you can hide.

The America you and your forefathers knew is coming to an end thanks to the Illuminati controlled secret government, and now they want America to become a Third World Nation ruled by a Fascist Police State, under their dictatorial control.

This obviously cannot be achieved if America stays the way it is with many still being relatively well off, and still possessing firearms. Only the people of America can stop the coming American Holocaust from occurring.

In America alone there are over 120 Deep Underground Military Bases situated under most major cities, USAF Bases, US Navy Bases and US Army Bases, as well as underneath FEMA Military Training Camps and DHS control centers.

There are also many Deep Underground Military Bases under Canada. Almost all of these bases are over 2 miles underground and have diameters ranging from 10 miles up to 30 miles across!

They have been building these bases day and night, unceasingly, since the 1940s. These bases are basically large cities underground connected by high-speed magneto-levity trains. Several books have been written on this activity.

The average depth of these bases is over a mile, and they again are basically whole cities underground. They have nuclear powered laser drilling machines that can drill a tunnel seven miles long in one day. (Note: The September, 1983 issue of Omni (Pg. 80) has a color drawing of 'The Subterrene,' the Los Alamos nuclear-powered tunnel machine that burrows through the rock, deep underground, by heating whatever stone it encounters into molten rock.)

The Black Projects sidestep the authority of Congress, which as we know is illegal. There is much hard evidence out there. Many will react with fear, terror and paranoia, but you must snap out of it and wake up from the brainwashing the media pumps into your heads all day long.

Are you going to be a rabbit in the headlights, or are you going to stand up and say enough is enough? The US Government through the NSA, DOD, CIA, DIA, ATF, ONI, US Army, US Marine Corp, FEMA and the DHS has spent in excess of 12 trillion dollars building the massive, covert infrastructure for the coming One World Government and New World Religion over the past 40 years.

There is the Deep Underground Military Base underneath Denver International Airport, which is over 22 miles in diameter and goes down over 8 levels. It's no coincidence that the CIA is relocating the headquarters of its domestic division, which is responsible for operations in the United States, from the CIA's Langley headquarters to Denver.

Constructed in 1995, the government and politicians were hell bent on building this airport in spite of it ending up vastly over budget. Charges of corruption, constant construction company changes, and mass firings of teams once they had built a section of their work was reported so that no "one" group had any idea what the blueprint of the airport was.

Not only did locals not want this airport built nor was it needed, but everything was done to make sure it was built despite that. Masonic symbols and bizarre artwork of dead babies, burning cities and women in coffins comprise an extensive mural as well as a time capsule – none of which is featured in the airport's web site section detailing the unique artwork throughout the building.

Denver International Airport serves as a cover for the vast underground facilities that were built there. There are reports of electronic/magnetic vibrations which make some people sick and cause headaches in others.

There are acres of fenced-in areas which have barbed wire pointing into the area as if to keep things in, and small concrete stacks that resemble mini-cooling towers rise out of the acres of nowhere to apparently vent underground levels.

The underground facility is 88.3 square mile deep. Basically this Underground Base is 8 cities on top of each other!

The holding capacity of such leviathanic bases is huge. These city-sized bases can hold millions and millions of people, whether they are mind controlled, enslaved NWO World Army Soldiers or innocent and enslaved surface dwellers from the towns and cities of America and Canada.

There is Dulce Base, in New Mexico. Dulce is a small town in northern New Mexico, located above 7,000 feet on the Jicarilla Apache Indian Reservation. There is only one major motel and a few stores.

It's not a resort town and it is not bustling with activity. But Dulce has a deep, dark secret. The secret is harbored deep below the brush of Archuleta Mesa. Function: Research of mind related functions, genetic experiments, mind control training and re-programming.

There are over 3000 real-time video cameras throughout the complex at high-security locations (entrances and exits).

There are over 100 secret exits near and around Dulce. Many around Archuleta Mesa, others to the south around Dulce Lake and even as far east as Lindrith. Deep sections of the complex connect into natural cavern systems.

Level 1 – garage for street maintenance. Level 2 – garage for trains, shuttles, tunnel-boring machines and disc maintenance. Level 3 – everyone is weighed, in the nude then given a jump suit uniform.

The weight of the person is put on a computer I.D. card each day. Any change in weight requires a physical exam and X-ray.

Level 4 – Human research in 'paranormal' areas – mental telepathy, mind control, hypnosis, remote viewing, astral traveling – etc.

The technology is apparently here to allow them to know how to manipulate the 'Bioplasmic Body' Development of a laser weapon that can remotely cause burns and discomfort on its target.

They can lower your heartbeat with Deep Sleep 'Delta Waves,' induce a static shock, then reprogram, Via a Brain-Computer link. Level 5 -security is severe. Armed guards patrol constantly, and in addition to weight sensitive areas there (are) hand print and eye print stations.

Here, is the device that powers the transfer of atoms. Level 6 – Level 6 is privately called 'Nightmare Hall'. It holds the genetic labs. Experiments done on fish, seals, birds, and mice that are vastly altered from their original forms.

Then there is the Greenbrier Facility, in White Sulphur   Springs, West Virginia under the Greenbriar Resort. The Continuity of Government facility intended since 1962 to house the United States Congress, code-named Casper, is located on the grounds of the prestigious Greenbrier resort.

The bunker is beneath the West Virginia wing, which includes a complete medical clinic. Construction of the facility, which began in 1959, required 2.5 years and 50,000 tons of concrete.

The steel-reinforced concrete walls of the bunker, which is 20 feet below ground, are 2 feet thick. The facility includes separate chambers for the House of Representatives and the Senate, as well as a larger room for joint sessions.

These are located in the "Exhibit Hall" of the West Virginia Wing, which includes vehicular and pedestrian entrances which can be quickly sealed by blast doors. They don't even hide this one, and it's even a tourist attraction.

The Underground vault was built to meet the needs of a Congress-in-hiding – in fact the hotel is a replica of the White House. The underground area has a chamber for the Senate, a chamber for the House and a massive hall for joint sessions.

Although the hotel says it gives tours of the 112,000 square area daily, the installation still stands at the ready, its operators still working under cover at the hotel. The secrecy that has surrounded the site has shielded it both from public scrutiny and official reassessment.

Most Americans will not believe that an American Holocaust will happen until they see it happening with their own eyes.

Till then, it is just another strange conspiracy theory for them to laugh at. This is no laughing matter.

When it happens, it will be to late to stop it. Then President Bush said he would "use foreign troops" on the streets of America if another Islamic terrorist attack occurs, because there may not be enough US Military personnel to cope with the massive urban chaos and panic that will obviously ensue if it occurs.

Also, the US Government has been involved covertly in the creation of an army of loyal, brainwashed soldiers of the future. They will have cybernetic and microchip implants and will fight anywhere in the world, without question, with total loyalty and without hesitation or fear.

These soldiers were created at Brookhaven National Laboratories BNL, the National Ordinance Laboratories NOL and the Massachussetts Institute of Technology MIT, and covertly transferred under DOD and NSA control and planning.

Many of these soldiers are stationed in the Deep Underground Military Bases like the one under Denver International Airport. All of this information has been researched, and it has taken much effort to fit it together properly.

There are many mag-lev subterraenean train networks that stretch from the these complexes and go out to other underground bases. All soldiers working in these bases are microchipped and under total Psychotronic Mind Control.

Of the missing "Milk Carton People" that the FBI used to post on milk cartons, some were taken to these underground bases for genetic experimentation, microchipping, psychotronic mind control and cybernetic implantations for future use as brainwashed soldiers of the NWO.

Every year in America hundreds of thousands of people go missing. The creation of a total Global Fascist Police State by the Illuminati will happen if we do not all wake up and see what is happening.

I find it amazing that so many Americans, Scandanavians and Western Europeans refuse to believe that there are millions of UNISF and UNMNTF Troops in America. Under the Partnerships For Peace Program PFPP set up by President Bill Clinton in early 1993, thousands of troops a month have been coming into America.

These Fascist criminals parade as our friends and leaders, while stripping away democratic rights that will be replaced with a Corporatist and Fascist dictatorship, unless people, and especially Americans, wake up now. Here are the locations of some Deep Underground Military Bases in America:

ALASKA

1. Brooks Range, Alaska
2. Delta Junction, Alaska 2a. Fort Greeley, Alaska. In the same Delta Junction area.

ARIZONA

1. Arizona (Mountains) (not on map) Function: Genetic work. Multiple levels 2. Fort Huachuca, Arizona (also reported detainment camp) Function: NSA Facility

2. Luke Air Force Base

3. Page, Arizona Tunnels to: Area 51, Nevada Dulce base, New Mexico

4. Sedona, Arizona (also reported detainment camp) Notes: Located under the Enchantment Resort in Boynton Canyon. There have been many reports by people in recent years of "increased military presence and activity" in the area.

5. Wikieup, Arizona Tunnels to: Area 51

6. Yucca (Mtns.), Arizona

CALIFORNIA

1: 29 Palms, California Tunnels to: Chocolate Mts., Fort Irwin, California (possibly one more site due west a few miles)

2: Benicia, California

3. Catalina Island, California Tunnels to: I was told by someone who worked at the Port Hueneme Naval Weapons Division Base in Oxnard that they have heard and it is 'common rumor' that there is a tunnel from the base to this Island, and also to Edwards Air Force Base, possibly utilizing old mines. .

4. China Lake Naval Weapons Testing Center

5. Chocolate Mountains, California Tunnels to: Fort Irwin, California

6. Death Valley,California Function: The entrance to the Death Valley Tunnel is in the Panamint Mountains down on the lower edge of the range near Wingate Pass, in the bottom of an abandoned mine shaft. The bottom of the shaft opens into an extensive tunnel system

7. Deep Springs, California Tunnels to: Death Valley, Mercury, NV, Salt Lake City

8. Edwards AFB, California Function: Aircraft Development – antigravity research and vehicle development Levels: Multiple Tunnels to: Catalina Island Fort Irwin, California Vandenburg AFB, California Notes: Delta Hanger – North Base, Edwards AFB, Ca. Haystack Buttte – Edwards, AFB,

Ca.

9. Fort Irwin, California (also reported detainment camp) Tunnels to: 29 Palms, California Area 51, Nevada Edwards AFB. California Mt. Shasta, California

10. Helendale, California Function: Special Aircraft Facility Helendale has an extensive railway/shipping system through it from the Union Pacific days which runs in from Salt Lake City, Denver, Omaha, Los Angeles and Chicago

11. Lancaster, California Function: New Aircraft design, anti-gravity engineering, Stealth craft and testing Levels: 42 Tunnels To: Edwards A.F.B., Palmdale

12. Lawrence-Livermore International Labs, California The lab has a Human Genome Mapping project on chromosome #19 and a newly built $1.2 billion laser facility

13. Moreno Valley, California Function unknown

14. Mt. Lassen, California Tunnels to: Probably connects to the Mt. Shasta main tunnel.

15. Mt. Shasta. Function: Genetic experiments, magnetic advance, space and beam weaponry. Levels: 5 Tunnels to: Ft. Irwin, California North

16. Napa, California Functions: Direct Satellite Communications, Laser Communications. Continuation of Government site. Levels: Multi-level Tunnels to: Unknown Notes: Located on Oakville Grade, Napa County, Ca. 87 Acres

17. Needles, California Function unknown

18. Palmdale, California Function: New Aircraft Design, anit-gravity research

19. Tehachapi Facility (Northrop, California – Tejon Ranch Function: Levels: 42 Tunnels to: Edwards, Llona and other local areas Notes: 25 miles NW of Lancaster California, in the Tehachapi mountains.

20. Ukiah, California Function unknown

COLORADO

1. Near Boulder, Co. in the mountains
Function unknown

2. Cheyenne Mountain -Norad -Colorado

Springs, Colorado Function: Early Warning systems – missile defense systems – Space tracking Levels: Multiple Tunnels to: Colorado Springs, Function: Early warning systems, military strategy, satellite operations Levels: Multiple NORAD is a massive self-sustaining 'city' built inside the mountain Tunnels to: Creede, Denver, Dulce Base, Kinsley.

3. Creede, Colorado Function unknown Tunnels to: Colorado Springs, Colorado – Delta, Colorado – Dulce Base, New Mexico

4. Delta, Colorado Function unknown Tunnels to: Creede Salt Lake, Utah

5. Denver International Airport (also a detainment camp) Function: Military research, construction, detainment camp facilities Levels: 7 reported Tunnels to: Denver proper, Colorado and Rocky Mountain "safehousing", Colorado Springs, Colorado (Cheyenne Mtn.)

6. Falcon Air Force Base, Falcon, Colorado Function: SDI, Satellite Control Levels: Multiple Tunnels to: Colorado Springs, possibly more.

7. Fort Collins, Colorado Function: Suspect high precision equipment manufacturing for space.

8. Grand Mesa, Colorado Function unknown

9. Gore Range Near Lake, west of Denver, Co. Function: Library and Central Data Bank

10. San Juan Valley, Colorado Hidden beneath and in an operating Buffalo Ranch Function unknown

11. Telluride, Colorado Function unknown

12. University of Denver, Co (Boulder area) Function: Genetics, geology/mining as related to tunneling and underground construction.

13. Warden Valley West of Fort Collins, CO Function Unknown Tunnels to: Montana

GEORGIA

Dobbins Air Force Base, Marrietta GA Function: test site for plasma and antigravity air craft, experimental crafts and weapons

INDIANA

Kokomo, Indiana Function Unknown Notes:

for years people in that area have reported a "hum" that has been so constant that some have been forced to move and it has made many others sick.

It seems to come from underground, and "research" has turned up nothing although it was suggested by someone that massive underground tunneling and excavating is going on, using naturally occurring caverns, to make an underground containment and storage facility.

KANSAS

1. Hutchinson, Kansas Function unknown
Tunnels to: Kinsley, Nebraska

2. Kansas City, Kansas Function unknown
Notes: Entrance near Worlds of Fun

3. Kinsley, Kansas Function unknown
Tunnels to: Colorado Springs, Colorado; Hutchinson, Kansas; Tulsa Kokoweef Peak, SW California Notes: Gold stored in huge cavern, blasted shut. Known as the "midway city" because it's located halfway between New York and San Francisco.

MARYLAND

Edgewood Arsenal, Maryland (from Don)
Martins AFB, Aberdeen Proving Ground,
Maryland

MASSACHUSETTS

Maynard MA, FEMA regional center.
Wackenhut is here too.

MONTANA

Bozeman, Mont. Function: Genetics

NEVADA

Area 51 – Groom Lake – Dreamland – Nellis
Air Force Base Area 51 was said to exist only
in our imaginations until Russian satellite
photos were leaked to US sources and it's
amazing how you can get photos all over of it
now, even posters.

They've been busy little bees building this
base up. Function: Stealth and cloaking
Aircraft research & development. 'Dreamland
(Data Repository Establishment and
Maintenance Land) Elmint (Electromagnetic
Intelligence), Biological weapons research and
genetic manipulation/warfare storage, Cold
Empire, EVA, Program HIS (Hybrid
Intelligence System),BW/CW; IRIS (Infrared

Intruder Systems), Security: Above ground cameras, underground pressure sensors, ground and air patrol

2. Blue Diamond, Nevada Function unknown

3. Fallon Air Force Base area (the flats, near Reno) "American City" restricted military sites southwest of Fallon

4. Mercury, Nevada Function unknown

5. Tonopah, Nevada Function unknown 69: San Gabriel (mountains) On Western side of Mojave Desert Function unknown Notes: Heavy vibrations coming from under the forest floor which sounds like geared machinery. These vibrations and sounds are the same as heard in Kokomo, Indiana and are suspected underground building/tunneling operations.

NEW MEXICO

1. Albuquerque, New Mexico (AFB) Function unknown Levels: Multiple Tunnels to: Carlsbad, New Mexico Los Alamos, New Mexico Possible connections to Datil, and other points.

2. Carlsbad, New Mexico Functions:

Underground Nuclear Testing Tunnels to:
Fort Stockton, Texas. Roswell

3. Cordova, New Mexico Function unknown

4. Datil, New Mexico Function unknown
Tunnels to: Dulce Base

5: Dulce Base, New Mexico. Tunnels to:
Colorado Springs, Colorado Creed, Colorado
Datil, N.M. Los Alamos. Page, Arizona Sandia
Base Taos, NM.

Dulce underground alien facility:

6. Los Alamos, New Mexico Functions:
Psychotronic Research, Psychotronic
Weapons Levels: Multiple Tunnels to: ALB
AFB, New Mexico Dulce, New Mexico
Connections to Datil,Taos

7. Sandia Base, New Mexico Functions:
Research in Electrical/magnetic Phenomena
Levels: Multiple Tunnels to: Dulce Base
Notes: Related Projects are studied at Sandia
Base by 'The Jason Group' (of 55 Scientists).
They have secretly harnessed the 'Dark Side
of Technology' and hidden the beneficial
technology from the public.

8. Sunspot, NM Function unknown

9. Taos, New Mexico Function unknown
Tunnels to: Dulce, New Mexico; Cog, Colorado
Notes: Several other sidelines to area where
Uranium is mined or processed.

10. White Sands, NM Function: Missile
testing/design Levels: Seven known

NEW HAMPSHIRE

There may be as many as three underground
installations in New Hampshire's hills,
according to reports.

NEW YORK

New York, New York Function unknown
Tunnels to: Capitol Building, D.C.

OHIO

Wright-Patterson Air Force Base – Dayton,
Ohio Function: Air Force Repository.
Rumored to house stealth technology and
prototype craft

OREGON

1. Cave Junction, Oregon Function: Suspected

Underground UFO Base Levels: At least one Notes: Suspected location is in or near Hope Mountain. Near Applegate Lake, Oregon, just over into California. Multiple shafts, access areas to over 1500 feet depth. Built using abandoned mine with over 36 known miles of tunnels, shafts.

2. Crater Lake, Oregon Tunnels: possible to Cave Junction

3. Klamath Falls, Oregon

4. Wimer, Oregon (Ashland Mt. area) Function: Underground Chemical Storage Levels: At least one

PENNSYLVANIA

Raven Rock, Pa (near Ligonier) Function: working back up underground Pentagon – sister site of Mt. Weather Notes: 650' below summit, 4 entrances.

TEXAS

1. Calvert, Texas Function unknown

2. Fort Hood, Texas (also reported detainment camp) Levels: Multiple

3. Fort Stockton, Texas Function: Unknown
Tunnels to: Carlsbad, New Mexico

UTAH

1. Dugway, Utah Function: Chemical Storage,
Radiation storage.

2. Salt Lake City Mormon Caverns Function:
Religions archives storage. Levels: Multiple
Tunnels to: Delta, Colorado & Riverton,
Wyoming

VIRGINIA

Mount Poney – Near Culpepper, Virginia
Function unknown

WASHINGTON

1. Mt. Rainier, Washington Function
unknown. Levels: Multiple Tunnels to:
Unknown Yakima Indian Reservation
Function unknown Notes: Southeast of
Tacoma Washington, on the Reservation, in
an area 40 by 70 miles. Unusual sounds from
underground (Toppenish Ridge). Low flying
Silver Cigar shaped craft seen to disappear
into the Middle fork area of Toppenish creek.

Washington DC: The Function: Part of a

massive underground relocation system to house select government and military personnel in the event of cataclysmic event. Tunnels to: New York City; Mt. Weather.

WEST VIRGINIA

Greenbrier Facility, White Sulphur Springs, West Virginia under the Greenbriar Resort.

WYOMING

Riverton, Wyoming Function unknown
Tunnels to: Salt Lake, Utah Denver, Colorado.

Mormon Illuminati Underground City?

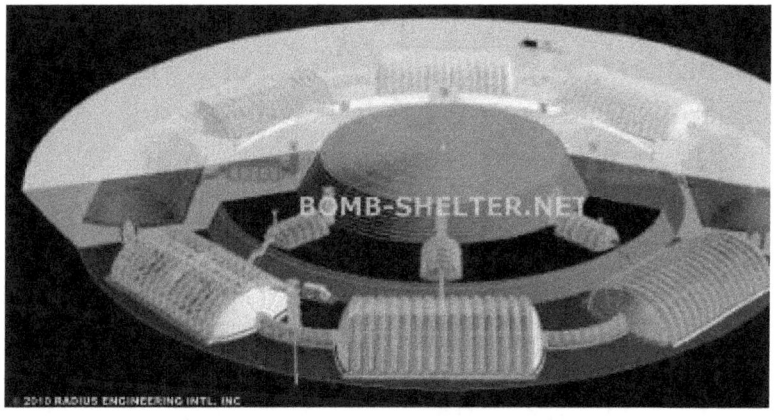

Shelter Price Military Model: $160,530,800
U.S. Dollars

The above "military grade" underground
bunker can hold 2,000 people, up to 60 months
worth of food, and has its underground power
system. It also has its own air/water
purification system and guaranteed to protect
against nuclear, chemical and biological
agents. The total cost is 160 million dollars.

The Mormon Illuminati funded "City Creek
Center" project, with a budget that could be as
high as $8-10 billion, has very little
investment going above ground (source).
Probably staying pretty close its $300 million
dollar initial budget. Which means that one of
two things is going on:

1. Its a money laundering operation with a
construction project as its front. In which
case, some vigilant citizen could make
millions of dollars by reporting it to the
Internal Revenue Service (They pay a 10%
finders fee on any uncollected income taxes).

2. The Mormon Illuminati have partnered
with the Mormon Church to build an

underground city for the coming apocalypse.

I believe that the underground city makes more sense, considering how the project is being financed. According to President Gordon B Hinckley:

"We are now working on a major undertaking in Salt Lake City. It is imperative that we preserve the environment around Temple Square. This makes necessary a very large construction project. Tithing funds will not be used for this construction. The income from Church businesses, rents on the property, and other such sources make this possible."

Yet, in another statement he proclaimed that income from Church owned businesses would not sustain the Church for a very long time. This makes it highly unlikely that Church Investments are still behind this now multi-billion dollar development.

Which indicates that the multi-billion dollar project is now being funded by mostly private donations. This money would come from Mormon Illuminati familes like the Eccles (Federal Reserve, Planned Parenthood, Eugenics and Gay Rights), the Marriotts

(Gambling, Pornography and Alcohol), Mitt Romney (Olympics Cover-up, Hedge Funds, Neocon) and others.

The Illuminati are bringing about their "age of Lucifer" through destroying the current world order and building a new one on its ashes. Their program includes massive depopulation through:

1. World War III: A conflict between Islam, China and Russia vs. the United States, Israel, Canada and Western Europe.

2. Biological warfare.

3. Chemical Warfare

4. Nuclear Warfare

5. Economic collapse & Race Riots

Considering the amount of havoc they plan on unleashing on the earth's surface, an underground city in downtown Salt Lake makes a whole lot of sense. Before the cataclysm, they and their allies in the Mormon Church disappear to their "retreat". Meanwhile, MWMs (Mormons Without

Money) are learning for themselves the truth about God's existence as they prepare to meet their Maker.

CHAPTER THIRTEEN

The Next Battleground: The World's Food Supply

Picture the scene: A stranger walks into a small-town country store and accuses the owner of planting seeds in violation of his company's patent. When the store owner protests that he has done no such thing, the shady visitor leaves, all the while yelling that his company is big and will make the store owner pay. The company continues on with its harassment, utilizing private investigators who film farmers sowing their seeds, infiltrating community meetings and working informants. Some of the company's employees pretend to be surveyors. Others are more brazen and attempt to bully farmers into signing papers that will give them access to their private records. Sounds like the basis for a great screenplay, doesn't it? Unfortunately, it's really happening all across rural America. And the company we're talking about is none other than Monsanto. Filmmaker

Marie-Monique Robin has exposed Monsanto's evil empire in a new documentary that will probably never be aired on American television.

For years, farmers have been planting seeds in the spring for harvest in the fall. After the harvest, it is common practice for farmers to reclaim the seeds and clean them for replanting in the spring. The U.S. Patent and Trademark Office traditionally refused to award patents to seeds because they were considered a life form with far too many variables to patent. That all changed in 1980 when the U.S. Supreme Court, in a 5-4 decision, extended the patent law to cover "a live human-made microorganism." Although the ruling applied to a bacterium developed by a General Electric scientist to clean up oil spills, the precedent was set and the door was opened. Monsanto walked through that door and never looked back.

Monsanto developed and patented a genetically-engineered seed that resisted it's own weed killer, Roundup, giving farmers a convenient way to control weeds without harming their crops. However, what Monsanto gave itself is the gift that keeps on giving. Because the seeds are patented, farmers who buy these genetically-modified seeds must sign an agreement not to reuse the seed or sell it to other farmers, changing the face of farming forever. That means that farmers must now buy new seed every year. The increase in seed sales, combined with the increased sales of Roundup, has been a boon for Monsanto. Most of the farmers comply with the terms of the Monsanto contract. However, some farmers truly do not realize what they've gotten into and do not understand that they cannot reuse the seeds. Others will ignore the terms of the contract, preferring not to throw away perfectly good seeds. Even farmers who do not use Monsanto genetically-altered seeds and do not want to use them can fall victim to Monsanto's strong-arm tactics when water, wind or birds deposit the unwanted seeds in their fields. There is no way to visually tell one seed or plant from another; laboratory analysis is required. Monsanto will gladly send out its army of shady operatives to pull samples from farm fields for testing in order to protect its profits. If it is confirmed by laboratory analysis that the crop in your field came from Monsanto seeds, it won't matter that you did not put them there. It won't matter if you do not want them there. All that matters is that they are there, and Monsanto will do what it must do to protect its patent.

The ruthless pursuit of the world's food supply

During the 1990s, Monsanto declared itself a 'life sciences' company, spinning off its chemical and fibers operations. After yet another reorganization in 2002, it presented itself as an 'agricultural' company. While its PR machine positions Monsanto as a leader in the fight against world hunger, the simple fact is that it's all about profits. It's not like Monsanto is donating genetically modified seeds to combat world hunger. In fact, just the opposite is true. Monsanto knows that if it owns the seed market, it essentially controls the food supply. To that end, it has spent the last decade buying up over 50 GM and traditional seed companies around the globe. It squeezes its farmers for everything it can get, and it protects its patents with a ruthless pattern of litigation.

Since the mid-90s, Monsanto has sued 150 U.S. farmers for patent infringement. The most prevalent 'crime' involves the violation of a technology agreement that prevents farmers from saving seed from one season to plant the next season. Overseas, Monsanto's behavior has not been much better.

In 2005 a criminal investigation concluded that a Monsanto consultant visited the home of an Indonesian official and handed him an envelope containing a wad of hundred dollar bills. This bribe was in exchange for the official bypassing environmental impact studies on Monsanto's genetically-modified and highly toxic cotton plant. Under any other administration this criminal act would be prosecuted to the full extent of the law. However, Monsanto was allowed to cut a 'deferred prosecution agreement' with the Justice Department to avoid a criminal trial. Instead, Monsanto paid a million dollar fine and agreed to government oversight of its operations. Given the present administration, this amounts to no oversight at all, of course.

In India, an indigenous seed company, Navbharat Seeds Pvt. Ltd. of Gujarat brought a bollworm-resistant seed, Navbharat-151, to market in 1999. Navbharat-151 is preferred by Indian farmers because it is a conventional seed and was not produced by genetic engineering. In 2001, Monsanto claimed to have found its Bt. cotton gene in some of the fields of Navbharat-151 cotton and accused the Indian farmers of Gujarat of producing pirated seed via cross-fertilization of their Bollgard plant with Navbharat-151. However, the Monsanto seeds did not become commercially available in India until 2002. The only way this cross-fertilization could have occurred was through genetic pollution, or unless Monsanto was providing its seed illegally to Navbharat Seeds prior to 1999. This is just another example of the way Monsanto uses propaganda and public relations to attempt to extract royalties from unwitting farmers. It should be noted that Monsanto's field trials began illegally in India in 1998, and the company was taken to court by the Research Foundation for Science, Technology and Ecology (RFSTE) for violating the Indian Environmental Protection Act. Legal action notwithstanding, many Indian cotton farmers have fallen hopelessly into debt because of Monsanto's illegal and ruthless practices. Many have committed suicide.

On March 7, 2008, International Women's Day, dozens of Brazilian women occupied the research site at the Monsanto facility in Sao Paulo, destroying the greenhouse and Monsanto's experimental plots of genetically-modified corn. The protesters were members of the international farmers' organization, La Via Campesina, who took exception to the Brazilian government's decision to legalize Monsanto's genetically-modified Guardian® corn, just weeks after France banned it due to environmental concerns and potential human health risks. The farmers object to seed patenting because it keeps poor farmers in debt to the corporations owning the seed patents and takes away the farmers' freedom to keep and share seeds. Brazilian farmers also believe that Monsanto's GM crop threatens biodiversity and Brazil's native seed varieties, and violates the rights of small farmers and consumers by contaminating organic and conventional crops.

This is Monsanto's master plan. Introduce its genetically-modified seed and sit back while it contaminates fields grown with traditional seeds. Once that has happened, Monsanto claims their seeds have been pirated. It is not only happening in India and Brazil. It is happening in Mexico, where the origin for maize has been deeply contaminated by Monsanto's GM seeds, Africa and Paraguay. Monsanto's reach has even extended to Iraq, a country we have already devastated through war. One of L. Paul Bremer's final acts was to establish an order preventing farmers from reusing 'protected' (or patented) seeds. The world is easy to contaminate, but hard to police, so the next logical step for Monsanto, of course, was development of the so-called 'terminator' or 'suicide' seed.

In 2006, Monsanto purchased a company called Delta & Pine Land. Conveniently, this is the company that has been working with our own U.S. Department of Agriculture (USDA) on genetically engineered seeds since 1983, and one of the main projects has been the 'terminator' or 'suicide' seed. These seeds have been genetically modified to 'commit suicide' after one harvest season, preventing farmers from saving or reusing the seed. This would mean that Monsanto can save money because it will no longer need to employ its cadre of thugs to strong-arm farmers into submission.

How did Monsanto get where it is?

How did a company that manufactured Agent Orange (used as a defoliant during the Vietnam war), PCBs and dioxin, and left in its wake 50 known Superfund sites, come to control 90% of the world's GM seed market? The short answer is that it has always had more than enough help from the U.S. Government. In 2006, Monsanto donated $106,500 to federal candidates with 32% going to the Democrats and 68% to Republicans. While this number may seem insignificant, it's the approximately $4 million it spent on lobbying that helps them curry favor with the government.

Monsanto, more than any other U.S. Company, is a master at using the government's unethical 'revolving door' policy. In 1991, Michael Taylor, was appointed deputy commissioner of the U.S. Food & Drug Administration (FDA). He had previously been an attorney at Monsanto. While in his government position, Taylor made key decisions that allowed the government to approve GE crops without proper testing and consumer labeling, in spite of the fact that there were (and still are) serious concerns about their safety. Taylor then returned to Monsanto to work in 'long range planning.' He is just one of the many Monsanto employees who have conveniently found their way into government positions, and then returned to the private sector after accomplishing their tasks.

Because Monsanto successfully

prevented labeling of food packages, consumers do not know that 60-70% of the food on store shelves, including cereals, snack foods, and even baby foods, contain some type of genetically-modified ingredients. These ingredients also frequently turn up in animal feed. How safe are they? Because they were never appropriately tested, nobody really knows. Some of the potential problems include introduction of allergens and toxins into foods, antibiotic resistance, accidentally changing the nutrient content of crops and the creation of 'superweeds' and other environmental risks. Of these potential risks, allergens and toxins are the most dangerous.

While responsibility for regulation falls to the Environmental Protection Agency (EPA), the U.S. Department of Agriculture (USDA) and the FDA. However, industry experts say that the green light is given mostly by the companies developing the technology. It is no surprise, then, that Monsanto owns 90% of the domestic genetically-modified seed market. (The rest is split among other companies, including Dow Chemical and Syngenta AG.) The FDA has a unique policy for determining the safety of GM foods: Genetically-modified foods simply need to be 'substantially equivalent' to non-modified foods. This is hardly a scientific approach.

In the meantime, Monsanto's unregulated march to control the world food supply continues with its recent announcement of the purchase of Marmot SA, which operates Central America's largest corn seed company. This purchase will solidify Monsanto's position as the leading corn seed supplier to the Latin American and Central American regions. Monsanto's assault on the public food supply now moves to milk. Its synthetic Recombinant Bovine Growth Hormone, known as rBGH, has been banned for health reasons in every industrialized country except the United States, of course. Oakhurst Dairy of Maine, like many other milk suppliers, has been responding to the desire of American consumers and providing milk free of rBGH, and they have been labeling their containers as such. Monsanto sued Oakhurst to prevent them from telling their customers that the milk is free of the Monsanto chemical. Faced with intense pressure from a multinational corporation and rising legal costs, Oakhurst was forced to settle out of court.

In spite of this, Monsanto's ruthless

march to control the world's food supply continues unabated, financially devastating America's small family-owned farms, putting untested food on our shelves for unwitting Americans to consume, and generally wreaking worldwide havoc – Deb Della Piana.

Note: it is obvious to the author of this book and other Illuminati researchers that Monsanto is Illuminati controlled.

HEALTH SCANDAL - MONSANTO'S GMO PERVERSION OF FOOD

In the 2010 growing season Monsanto unleashed its latest Frankenfood experiment on the American and Canadian public, a new version of genetically mutated corn with eight abnormal gene traits called Genuity SmartStax corn. It is the culmination of an astonishing scandal that has been steadily building over the past decade. During this time Monsanto's mutated seeds have grown to 90% of the U.S. soy crop and 85% of the corn crop – and wheat is next on their agenda. Their efforts have been marked by corporate bullying and have drawn the attention of the Justice Department who is conducting an antitrust investigation. All the while they have been spending millions on lobbying to fast track their agenda before the American public even realizes what hit them. Monsanto is making an ominous power play to corner the worldwide market on food and seeds. In the process they are adversely altering the very nature of food itself.

Few people would eat Monsanto's "food" if they understood what it was or knew that they were eating it. President Obama and his family won't eat it. Neither did the Bush family. Even a Monsanto employee cafeteria rejects it. This is no laughing matter. Your health and the health of your children and grandchildren are at stake. It seems more like a scene from a horror flick than something happening in modern day America. Imagine your digestive tract turned into a Roundup Ready herbicide factory and other warped genetic signals slowly and progressively rotting away your health. Unlike acute food poisoning from infectious E.coli, it is a slow and insidious poisoning.

Why GMO Food is Dangerous

Monsanto's GMO (genetically modified organism) technology inserts non-food genes, genes from other species, into the DNA of food, altering the very nature of food itself. In some cases these genes make the crops more tolerant to the Roundup Ready herbicide made by Monsanto and in other cases the genes abnormally cause the DNA of food cells to produce toxic proteins that act as pesticides.

Most people are not comfortable with the concept of altering the nature of food in a grand genetic experiment with unknown consequences. The idea of food producing its own internal toxin is equally abhorrent. After all, who wants to eat toxic food? Even fewer trust this technology in the hands of Monsanto, a company with a history of blatant disregard for human health. It was Monsanto that knowingly poisoned the planet with toxic PCBs.

The process of making GMO seeds also poses health risks. Viral promoter genes are used during this production process and become part of the DNA mix, posing a risk for new types of viral disease. An unintended side-effect of this production technology is chronic activation or suppression of normal genes in the modified plants. This alters the actual nutrient structure of food and the function of the proteins within that food – a very serious matter.

The entire process of producing GMO seeds is also unpredictable. It creates multiple random genetic events in every food cell invaded by the mutant genes. Because each gene doesn't just do one thing and is highly interactive with other genes, the production of GMO food is not consistent and therefore safety cannot be guaranteed – especially when you understand that our scientific knowledge of gene interdependencies is in its infancy.

Eating food that is mutated by other non-food species is a grand experiment to say the least. GMO mutants can transfer to the living bacteria in your digestive tract, as has been shown in animal experiments. This can adversely change the way your gut bacteria behave so that they create pesticides and become more resistant to your immune system and medical treatments. If the GMO mutants were to transfer to an existing infection in your digestive tract then it could create your own superbug.

Because the proteins in GMO food are

structurally different than normal food they significantly increase the risk for allergy. Allergy is one form of inflammation that is likely to result from GMO food, but there are many other potential sources. These include the mis-metabolism of the food, the inherent toxicity of the food, and the pesticide residues on the food. These inflammatory problems of GMO food will additively contribute to other forms of inflammation such as pollution and stress and add to the total inflammation burden sets the stage for many diseases. It is likely that GMO food will have a significant impact on pregnancy problems and developmental problems in children. At this time nobody can rule out GMO as a possible causative factor in Autism, as the rates of both have risen together. A recent re-evaluation of data provided by Monsanto showed that various types of GMO corn caused significant inflammatory organ damage to rats.

It has now been shown that the health consequence of eating high amounts of Roundup Ready residue that is being sprayed in ever-higher amounts on GMO crops is the disruption of your endocrine system. A recent study shows that these residues of Roundup Ready are highly interactive with sex hormones and significantly disrupt their function.

A 2008 Austrian government study showed that feeding GMO corn to mice for multiple generations resulted in fertility issues and weakened kidneys, as well as changes in metabolic pathways involved with inflammation, cholesterol, and protein. Here is a link to the 105 page report.

GMO crops are also drastically and adversely altering soil quality. In fact, soil animals such as earthworms are now found to have incorporated GMO mutant corn genes into their cells. This finding is of extreme importance to potential human health problems. There is certainly nothing preventing this from happening to humans.

For more information on the devastating health consequences of consuming GMO foods read Jeffrey Smith's books, Seeds of Deception and Genetic Roulette."

You may be wondering the obvious; if GMOs are so dangerous to eat then why are they allowed in the food supply?

Corporate Cronyism - A Corrupt FDA Places

the Public in Danger

We now know that FDA scientists originally working on the issue of the safety of GMO food had considerable concerns that included allergies, toxins, adverse nutritional effects, and new diseases. They urged long-term studies but were ignored by FDA management who instead decided that GMO food was "substantially equivalent" to normal food. In 1992 these managers issued the following policy statement in the Federal Register, "The agency is not aware of any information showing that foods derived by these new methods differ from other foods in any meaningful or uniform way." In retrospect, that policy, which stands to this day, was a flat out lie and a treasonous betrayal of the public trust.

Court cases have forced into public view the documents expressing the concerns of the FDA scientists. You can read them all at this link to the BioIntegrity.Org website. In fact, rushing GMO foods to market also represents a serious breach of scientific integrity by the overall research community.

Today, the FDA is a world leader in proteomic technology, the advanced analysis of protein structure and function. Italian researchers using proteomics have already proven beyond any question that GMO food is so genetically different from normal food that it cannot possibly be considered substantially equivalent. Certainly the FDA could discover this fact for themselves in a matter of hours. Why are FDA scientists in handcuffs and not taking action?

Part of the FDA management team's culture of corruption is a revolving door with the various companies they are supposed to be regulating, the very definition of corporate cronyism. These shenanigans have had the net effect of the FDA acting primarily as a police force bully representing various powerful lobbies that buy protection and marketing favors, while stomping on the rights of the little guys like organic family farms and consumers. In the case of food, Monsanto wins the gold medal for influence pedaling at the expense of human health.

One of the more egregious examples of cronyism is Michael Taylor. He was an FDA staff lawyer and Executive Assistant to the FDA Commissioner from 1976 to 1981. From 1981 to 1991 he worked at the law firm of King and Spaulding, acting as Monsanto's lawyer and lobbyist. He was a major proponent for overturning the Delaney Clause, a 1958 law prohibiting the introduction of known carcinogens to processed foods, a law Monsanto hated and which was eventually overturned by Clinton in 1996. His main responsibility during this time was gaining regulatory approval of Monsanto's genetically modified cancer-causing bovine growth hormone (rBGH).

To complete his efforts on the bovine growth hormone issue Taylor went back to work for the FDA in 1991 with the title Deputy Commissioner for Policy at the Food and Drug Administration. He was directly responsible for writing the FDA policy on "substantial equivalence" which initially ushered in the rBGH era and to this day enables Monsanto to market its GMO mutated food with no appropriate oversight by the FDA as to safety. He also formulated policy that prevented milk producers from informing consumers that their milk was free of bovine growth hormone – intentionally preventing consumers from being able to tell what was in the milk product they were consuming.

After accomplishing his dirty work, he left the FDA in 1994 and went to work for Monsanto as Vice President for Public Policy, working on Monsanto's long range plans. More recently, he became a Senior Fellow at Resources for the Future (RFF) and Director of the Risk, Resources and Environmental Management division. In this role, he strategized how to get Monsanto's GMO crops into Africa, working closely with the Bill and Melinda Gates Foundation and the Rockefeller Foundation. He also worked closely with the Bush Administration, and is the point man in helping an elite agenda to spread GMO seeds and biotech dependence around the world.

You guessed it – now he is back at the FDA in a new position the Obama Administration created – Senior Advisor to the Commissioner, working primarily on issues of food safety! "I am pleased to welcome Mike Taylor back to the FDA," Commissioner of Food and Drugs Margaret A. Hamburg, M.D., said in announcing Taylor's appointment. "His expertise and leadership on food safety issues will help the agency to develop and implement the prevention based strategy we need to ensure the safety of the food we eat."

As Monsanto, in anti-competitive collusion with Dow, takes their new GMO toxic and mutated corn to market, stacked with eight genes, it should come as no surprise that absolutely no safety testing is being required by the FDA. Never before have there been eight genes altered simultaneously within the cells of food. One gene is bad enough. Three is horrendous. But eight?

The fact that the FDA is not requiring extensive safety testing by independent sources of this highly unpredictable and dangerous technology is unthinkable. It is a grim day when the fox is in charge of the henhouse.

There Is No Good Reason for Monsanto's GMOs

If you listen to Monsanto and their business cohorts such as Cargill, they state they are trying to feed the world. In reality, the world could eliminate Monsanto's mutated food tomorrow and it would be a better place. It could also do without Cargill acting as an unregulated food banker, profiting on the manipulation of food sales at the expense of farmers in a way that is every bit as bad as the worst of Wall Street. There is no need for Monsanto's GMO mutated seeds. They offer no advantages. It is an industry being propped up by unelected bureaucrats and elected officials on the receiving end of Monsanto's multi-million dollar lobbying operation.

Michael Taylor is one example of corporate crony influence, there are many others. The USDA is profiting from Monsanto's seeds that cannot be used the next growing season (the Terminator aspect of the problem). The EPA's failure to regulate the amounts of Roundup Ready used on food is yet another scandal. It's all about profits and control – while undermining the world's farmers and the biodiversity and sustainability of crops.

Contrary to the Monsanto and Cargill propaganda, GMO technology does not increase crop yields, as has been fully documented in the Union of Concerned Scientists report titled Failure to Yield. And GMO crops are very bad for the carbon footprint.

The fact that the Obama administration is actively forwarding Monsanto's efforts should be a grave concern to every American.

Of course, the last 16 years of Clinton and Bush also did everything in their power to help Monsanto. No wonder Americans are fed up. Politicians in both parties are beholden to the golden idol, not the best health interests of its citizens – Byron J, Richards.

Note: It is obvious to the author of this book, and other Illuminati researchers, that Genetically Modified Food is just another Illuminati plot to eventually kill millions of people. No one knows the long time results of GMO's. Personally, I eat only organic food and drink only organic milk. It costs a bit more, but it is certainly safer. Some folks I know have a garden and plant only organic seeds.

CHAPTER FOURTEEN

The Illuminati

Exclusive Interview with an Ex-Illuminati
Programmer/Trainer

Illuminati History and Future

Q: I've received some Neo-Nazi-white power-invitations through e-mail. I've read some of the stuff and (to put it short) they argue with considerable elegance - backed up with historical "facts"- that the Illuminati, of course, is a Jewish Conspiracy, and that Hitler was "on to them", and we all know what happened next. My simple question: Is the Illuminati a JEWISH conspiracy?

Svali: My answer: absolutely not. In fact, Hitler and his people (especially Himmler and

Goebbels) were top Illuminists. The Illuminati are racist in the extreme, and as a child, I was forced to play "concentration camp" both on my farm in Virginia, and also in Europe in isolated camps in Germany.

The Jews historically fought against the occult. See Deuteronomy and the Old Testament for how God through the Jewish people tried to cleanse the land of the occult groups that were operating there, such as those who worshipped Baal, Ashtarte, and other Canaanite and Babylonian gods.

Since the Illuminati trace their roots to these ancient fertility deities, they also have an inground antithesis to the Jewish race. Also, I would never trust literature sent to me by Neo-Nazi or any extremist hate groups, since they are founded on the tenets of racism, egalitarianism, the concept of a master race, and other things that are also espoused strongly by the Illuminati and many other occult groups. Simply put, this group was lying to you, and counting on your not knowing that Nazism was founded by German Illuminists.

Q: The dream of someone wanting to rule the world is nothing new, obviously. History is littered with failed attempts to conquer the world and subjugate the population. How old is the dream for the 'NEW WORLD ORDER' per se, by the Illuminati?

Svali: The Illuminati themselves teach that they have been around for centuries and centuries, even during Roman times, and that Alexander the Great was one of their "prototypes" in the ancient world, as was Hitler in modern times. But the Illuminati as we know it today was formed in the 17th century (out of Catholic roots, ie. the Templar Knights and Roscicrucianism). The idea of a modern 'One World Order' became popular in the 1700's with the ideas of Weisshaupt and others, and they have been working towards this goal since the mid 18th century.

Q: Did the Illuminati manipulate societies throughout history, such as the Egyptian, Roman, British empire, etc. How far back does the history of the Illuminati stretch and were they always known as the Illuminati, or did they at times operate under different covers with the same goals?

Svali: The Illluminati say they date back to ancient Babylon on the Fields of Shinar around 3,900 B.C, give or take. But this is probably cult programming and boasting. They state that they are founded on the occult base of all ancient mystery religions and occult practices. But they actually seem to be descended from the Knights Templar during the medieval ages, and the Rosicrucians who were also founded back then. I myself have trouble knowing how much of the "cult history" I was taught as a child by my scholarship teachers was merely programming, and how much is accurate truth, so I cannot really be an objective source of information. Like any group, they tend to want to "idealize" their roots.

Q: Being as intelligent as they are, the Illuminati must know that empires and societies throughout history only lasted about 200 years, on average. Is this a natural life cycle, or was that duration and final downfall of empires coordinated? In other words, was the Illuminati responsible for failed empires? Did they purposely destroy societies and create new ones with the intention of securing a tighter grip on future governments?

Svali: During historical "set ups" that I saw as a child, used to teach the history of the group, supposedly behind the throne of all ancient and modern monarchies were Illuminist advisors and financing. They CLAIM to have manipulated history for the past 2,000 years. But I also believe that people have free choice, and that no one person or group can truly take into account the unpredictable: human nature and how they will respond.

I don't really believe they did all that they have claimed to. At the same time, in the last 200 years, they have certainly had a profound influence at the international and governmental level, based on what I saw and heard when in the group.

Q: Svali, you said Illuminists are working hard for those goals and looking forward to the final implementation of the 'glorious New Order', or world government, so that they can take part and be leaders in that society. At what point will the Illuminati be satisfied with their achievements, and what is their vision of that 'glorious New Order'? What shape, form or system will it have, what political infrastucture? Dictatorial, communist, democratic? Will there be an end to their struggle for global control?

Savli: I was taught that during the coming "Order" or Government, that it would at first be a heavily dictatorial and military government. This is why there is extensive training of covert military forces in all ranks, to implement this policy. Why? Because not everyone will welcome their "enlightened" rule, and there will be those who oppose them.

Their army is being trained in crowd control techniques and camps will be set up to send dissenters to. Think of Hitler's Germany, which was a prototype. The government will be highly authoritative and centralized in the Supreme World Council, with the national councils and regional councils under its control.

The implementation of a semi-marxist, or miltary socialism, will then follow (Marx was an Illuminist, and was told what to write in his treatises), co-ordinated under the umbrella of the regional and national councils. Financial power will be held at the national and international levels. People will be asked to work at reduced wages for the glory of serving the New Order, although compensation will be based on loyalty and performance as time goes on (much as in Marxist and Leninistic Russia).

Once the dissenters are subjugated and controlled, they believe that there will no longer be a need to try for world control. They will have it. They will then begin breeding programs to ensure that only the best and brightest reproduce; sterilization of those considered poor genetic specimens will begin. They are firm believers in "selective breeding", just as Hitler and his scientists were. It is sad, but true, that this is what they teach. Children will be tested for their psychic ability and will go through special teaching to increase their abilities, much as they do now covertly, only it will be open.

Q: Does the Illuminati have natural enemies or predators, or competitors with the same goals of global control?

Svali: Not that I know of. They are very aware of the Templar Knights, and OTO [Ordo Templi Orientis, a Catholic secret society that is a sister group to the Templar Knights and is involved in lots of occult and illegal activities as well], and while the two groups are split in some areas, they are very sympathetic and share resources with each other. The only true enemy that they see is the Christian church, which opposes all that they do. Because the Illuminati are based in occult spirituality, they despise any group that espouses Judaism or fundamental

Christianity as being their mortal enemies. This is because Christians engage in spiritual warfare that hurts their cause.

Q: What's your view on the role of China and Russia in light of the latest developments, the Russia-Sino political alignment against the U.S., given the insight you had when you were still part of the Illuminati?

Svali: Russia will be the military base and powerhouse of the group, since their military commanders (Illuminist) are considered the best in the world, and very, very disciplined. China, because of its roots in oriental occultism, and its large population, will also be considered a higher power than the US. But again, the real power will reside in Europe, according to what I was taught when part of the group.

China will administer the Eastern region and Russia the North. Again, I am sharing what I was taught, but please be aware that it may have been "programming". One of the most difficult tasks I have encountered since getting out has been to evaluate how much of what I was told is truth, and how much idealism and cult programming. I am NOT an authority on this group, and I held a very low position in it when I was part of it. I sat the leadership council on the San Diego metropolitan area for several years, but had little to do with the international arena.

The Illuminati
Exclusive Interview with an Ex-Illuminati Programmer/Trainer

The UN or 'Supreme World Council' -

Q: Svali, what role does and will the UN play in the future and how do you see this unfolding? What is their timeline?

A: The UN was created early in this century in order to help overcome one of the biggest barriers to a one world government necessary, if there is to be a military rule and dictatorship by the Illuminists. That barrier is the one of nationalism, or pride in one's country. This is why it was NOT a popular concept when first introduced, it took years of country bashing in the media and the destruction of any sense of national pride by a (not so subtle) media campaign over the years.

It's agenda? It is set up as a shadow, or forerunner, of the Supreme World Council that will represent every nation. Every ambassador to the UN has either done something to curry Illuminati favor and been rewarded, or is a political figurehead chosen to make the organization "look good".

The Illuminati and governmental leaders chose to create the UN early in the past century, and worked hard and against opposition to put it in place (FDR was their man in America who helped the American public accept it). Both he and Eleanor were staunch Illuminists. So is Shirley Temple Black. In fact, most of our presidents since the beginning of the past century have been either Illuminists, or agreed by oath to support their goals, in return for campaign funds and support. I believe it is impossible to win a presidential election in our country today without their backing. The Kennedy family were punished because they tried to disobey them. They were free thinkers, and too hard to "control".

The UN has a stated goal of world peace, and wants to incorporate under its fold military and peace-keeping functions. But in reality, giving this role to the UN weakens the individual military strength of nations, and encourages them to lean more and more on an external organization, making them less able to resist when the takeover occurs.

I was told that by the year 2020 the New Order would be openly revealed, BUT that may have been cult propaganda, and they are always changing dates. I personally believe that by the mid of this century, they will reveal themselves. This is just my opinion, though.

Q: What are the plans of the Illuminati for the Middle East and how will it affect the rest of the world? Will we see WWIII?

A: The conflict in the middle east is only to the advantage of the Illuminists. They HATE Israel, and hope one day to see it destroyed, and are biding their time. One of the olive branches offered by the UN when it takes over is that they will prevent war in the middle east, and this will be greeted with joy by many.

At the same time, the Illuminati covertly supply guns and funds to BOTH sides to keep the conflict fueled. They are very duplicious people. They used to funnel guns through the

USSR to Palestine, for example, in the name of promoting "friendliness" between the USSR and this state and other Arab nations. Then, the US Illuminists would help funnel guns to Israel, for the same reason.

These people love the game of chess, and see warfare between nations as creating an order out of chaos. The USSR is going to get stronger again. It has too strong a military both openly, and covertly (ALL Illuminati military trainers have visited Russia to learn from them) to sit quietly and quiesciently to the side. In the NWO, they will be stronger than us.

Want to hear the end of the world scenario the Illuminati taught me? It was cult propaganda, but this is how they believed the New Order would be ushered in:

There will be continued conflict in the Mideast, with a severe threat of nuclear war being the culmination of these hostilities.

An economic collapse that will devastate the economy of the US and Europe, much like the great depression.

One reason that our economy continues

limping along is the artificial supports that the Federal Reserve had given it, manipulating interest rates, etc. But one day, this won't work (or this leverage will be withdrawn on purpose) and the next great depression will hit. The government will call in its bonds and loans, and credit card debts will be called in. There will be massive bankruptcies nationwide. Europe will stabilize first, and Germany, France and England (surprise) will have the strongest economies, and will institute through the UN an international currency. Japan will also pull out, although their economy will be weakened.

Peacekeeping forces will be sent out by the UN and local bases to prevent riots. The leaders will reveal themselves, and people will be asked to make a pledge of loyalty during a time of chaos and financial devastation.

Doesn't sound pleasant, does it? I don't know the exact time frame for all of this, and wouldn't want to even guess. The good news is that if a person is debt-free, owes nothing to the government or credit debt, and can live self sufficiently, they may do better than other. I would invest in gold, not stocks, if I had the income. Gold will once again be the world standard, and dollars will be pretty useless (remember after the Civil War? Our money will be worth about what confederate money was after the collapse).

All this said, it could just be cult propaganda taught to me and others to frighten us. It may be that none of this will happen. I sincerely hope not. I also strongly believe that God is able to stay the hand of the wicked, and to take care of our nation and others, if we turn to Him.

Q: Overall, would you say the Illuminati are racist? I am asking this because their agenda seems to be very white supremist throughout history.

The Illuminati are racist, and have a very "Aryan" outlook. They believe strongly in the rule of the "pure" and "intelligent" by their definitions, and in their ceremonies, there will occasionally be minorities killed in ceremonies.

They are trying to breed a "genetically superior" race to rule, with their children and descendants. They are also followers of Plato's Republic, and believe that they will be the ones to usher in this "Utopian" rule with the NWO in their opinion. In their Utopia, the intelligentsia will rule, and the sheep like masses will follow their leaders (that is their view of the world; that the occult leaders are "enlightened' and intelligent, while the average person is a "sheep" to be led by the nose).

Q: Why would they allow a black leader to head the UN?

A: Because it is a temporarily politically expedient thing for them to do. They are liars, and will hold out a hand to a popular political figure, throwing them a figurehead role in one of their organizations, to make the UN look better, and as a group that promotes "interracial harmony" and "unity" and "peace".

The real leaders would never publicly allow their real feelings to show. The UN is a preparation, but it is not the real power in the world, and will be relatively unimportant when the NWO comes into being. The real councils will then step forward. But as a means of getting the general public to accept the idea of a "global community" and the "one world community" the UN is a stepping stone in their working towards the NWO.

Q: Do they have a population control agenda? I'm thinking specially in view of the AIDS plague in Africa. Could this be engineered by them?

A: I have heard reports that certain deadly viruses have been engineered by the Illuminati, but I doubt that HIV was. Why? Because so many of the leadership of the Illuminati are blatantly pedophilic and homosexual, the virus is rampant in parts of the US, and they would be endangering themselves as well. Most of the leadership that I knew were homosexuals in their night personas (myself included) and it was accepted as a lifestyle in that setting, and encouraged.

Also, the viruses that they are developing are ones that they are also engineering antidotes to, to protect leadership from the virus if an epidemic breaks out. I do know that there is some working on biological weapons by members of this group as a method of threatening population bases that don't embrace the "New Order" when revealed, this was discussed occasionally in leadership meetings. What state it is at this time, I couldn't say, since it has been several years since I was active in the group.

CHAPTER FIFTEEN

The Illuminati
Exclusive Interview with an Ex-Illuminati
Programmer/Trainer

Illuminati - CIA Connection - Russia & China

Svali: I just want you and your readers to know that I am NOT an Illuminati expert, nor do I want to be. I am only a survivor who was part of this group, in a lower management position locally. I did NOT rub elbows with the rich and famous, although I heard about things that occurred at higher levels (people do gossip even in the cult, they're still human beings).

There are other people who have come out and disclosed. I don't know them personally, but I have heard about them. One is Brice Taylor, in California and North Carolina (she lives part time in both places). Another is Neil Brick of SmartNews, he seems to be very real and believable and a nice person. Others are Caryn StarDancer, of Survivorship.org, and Annie McKenna (I think she even wrote a book about her experiences [ed. 'Paperclip Dolls'], it is quite good). There are others, and if you go to the Suite101.com site, there are links to resources and also survivor pages. Survivorship.org also has links.

Some survivors have self-published their stories on the web, to help the public know that this is going on. I am only one person among many who has come out to talk about my experiences, and my experiences are limited to what one person did in the Washington, DC area and the San Diego, Ca. area between 1957 and 1995. A person who was doing their job at the time, was very misguided, and who is now heartily sorry for the things that I once participated in.

Q: How do survivors remain anonymous after seeking help? Would the cult not go to extreme measures to find and silence programmers or members that have left the cult? To what ends would they go to shut you up?

A: At Suite 101, and in my book, I wrote a whole chapter on staying safe. Here's the URL for the Suite 101 article: Breaking Free of the Cult. It includes tips on staying safe.

Yes, they do try to re-contact people who get out. The first way they do this is through their family (remember they are transgenerational). My mother told me to "come back or die" four years ago, which triggered off lethal self destruct programming inside (I believe she was counting on my coming back, but she was wrong and I almost died. God spared my life). I then had to go in and dismantle it all. When I left, the head trainer was pretty arrogant. He had said I would be dead within 6 months if I remembered, because "no one could remember with what I put in her and live". Direct quote from Jonathan M., head trainer, and I hope he reads this article.

Second, a lot of people get abducted and re-accessed because they : phone their perps, go out alone at night (you wouldn't believe the stories I have heard from survivors who told me they went out at 2 or 3 am to the store, alone, walking down alleys. What were they thinking?

I helped one survivor get out three years ago, she was being harassed by the group, and was fighting back, she literally pulled a gun on a would-be abductor and he backed away (he had his gun out) when she asked him, "and who of the two of us do you think is the better shot?" She was an expert marksman. She stayed with me for 6 months, and is free of the group.

They usually do give up after awhile, and get tired of trying to pull people back. I could never live in San Diego, or DC, though. The chances of running into an old trainer or someone I knew would be too great. Instead, having physical distance (people in the cult in this state don't know me or care about me one way or the other) helps. I also have tons of accountability. These people like secrecy, and won't usually act out in public if someone is with people who aren't part of their group. I have heard of people being assassinated, which is one reason that I don't go on T.V., or speak publicly. I live very quietly and anonymously out here. MOST cult re-contact comes because the person re-contacts, though. The pull to go back is enormous at times, and has to be fought a lot, especially in the first years. To find out why someone would go back to their abusers, read my article on "Trauma Bonding: The Pull to the Perpetrator" at Suite 101.

Q: I want to get back to the Illuminati's political agenda. What is the connection between the CIA, FBI, and other secret services and the cult? To what degree are they infiltrated? And what is the real agenda of these secret services?

A: They are all infiltrated. I don't think everyone in these groups are Illuminists, but a lot of the leadership is. An example: my mother was friends with Sid Gottlieb, who was part of the CIA. The farm I grew up on was only about a half hour away from his home in Culpeper, Va. She also knew the Dulles family. A lot of the researchers in the CIA were part of it, and I visited Langley, Va. at intervals growing up. MK-Ultra was funded in part with Illuminati money. These people use the most sophisticated mind control techniques on their members, believe me.

When I was in San Diego, human experimentation was still going on. Jonathan and I were investigating the effects of certain drugs on inducing trance states and assisting with programming. We would take the data, and download it into a database (oh, yes, the cult is very technologically sophisticated) and then send it to Langley.

Many of the administrators and directors at the FBI are also Illuminists. The CIA helped bring over German scientists after WWII. Many of these were also Illuminati leaders in their own country, and they were welcomed with open arms by the U.S. group. They also funneled all information they were learning to the Illuminati.

Q: I assume if the U.S. political, banking, and military systems are all fairly well under Illuminati control this would then also be true for Eastern Europe, Russia and other communist bloc countries as well. What does this mean for relations between the West-East Axis? Was Russia, or the USSR at the time, ever the adversary it was made out to be, and was there a grand plan behind having Russia as an enemy?

A: Russia was never really a threat to us. Marxism was funded by the Illuminati, and espoused as a counterbalance to capitalism. The Illluminati believe strongly in balancing opposing forces, in the pull between opposites. They see history as a complex chess game, and they will fund one side, then another, while ultimately out of the chaos and division ..., they are laughing because they are ultimately beyond political parties. A top western financier will secretly meet with an eastern or Russian "adversary" during those years, and have a good laugh at how the "sheep" were being deluded. I am sharing here what I was taught, and also observed.

When DELPHI met with ORACLE in Europe, (these are the head training groups for the northern hemisphere and European continents) the Russian, German, French, British, Canadian, and US trainers all worked together. In fact, this is one reason why plurality of linguality is valued in the Illuminati. I had to learn six languages as a child, and learn to converse with people from around the world. They are truly an international group, and the group's agenda supercedes any nationalistic feelings. There is also a lot of trading back and forth of members in these groups. A Russian trainer might come to the US for awhile, complete a job, then go back, or vice-versa.

Q: China is starting to rattle their sabers and arming itself with nuclear weapons which are pointing at U.S. cities. Is all this occurring according to Illuminati agenda or is there still a fairly large 'uncertainty, random or x-factor' involved that is beyond the Illuminati's control?

A: I have been out for five years, so my information is "old news". But the military buildup of China is part of their plan. There are members of the group who are Asian, and very opportunistic. The Oriental Mafia groups are very much linked to Illuminati activity. The random factor in all of this is how the average citizen reacts. It can't be predicted, although Illuminati leadership will often invent different scenarios, and try to decide how they will act if the ordinary citizens react in an unexpected manner.

I was told that around 2020, the Illuminist agenda would be revealed openly. I don't know if this is accurate, or just propaganda that I was taught, or if they have changed this date since I was in the group.

Q: Svali, earlier you were talking about mind control victims and survivors that have come forward with their stories and publicized it. One of the more recent and high profile stories is the one of Cathy O'Brian [see links at www.vegan.swinternet.co.uk and www.trance-formation.com].

She seems to be more of a CIA mind control victim, which still sound very much like your own story, in terms of technology and technique. Do you think there could be an Illuminati connection?

A: As I mentioned before, the CIA and the Illuminati are definitely linked. The top leadership in the CIA are also Illuminati leaders. I mentioned Dulles and Gottlieb as men I knew personally as a child and young adult. The scientists that ran the MK-Ultra and other governmental mind control programs were Illuminists brought over from Nazi Germany. That's why you will find that mind control victims ALWAYS speak German or have a dissociated part that speaks with a German accent; they are mimicking their abusers, which is very, very common.

You could say that the CIA and the Illuminati are hand in glove companions. I know that the different Illuminati groups around the US also send data on the experiments they do to the central computer at Langley, Va. (oh, yes, human experimentation and mind control experiments are still ongoing, it didn't stop with WWII).

Exclusive Interview with an Ex-Illuminati
Programmer/Trainer

Lone Gunmen

Warning: this part contains some graphic
descriptions of assassin training and brutal
torture perpetrated on children by the
Illuminati.

Q: Svali, when you hear news stories about
the so-called 'lone gunman', or perfect patsy,
such as Timothy McVeigh, Lee Harvey
Oswald, Sirhan Sirhan, John Hinkley
(Reagan assassin), Eric Harris & Dylan
Klebold (Columbine High School) - and I'm
sure you could give us even more examples -
what is your feeling on this? Many of these
killers have links to the military, either
directly or through their family, and are
rumored to be mind control slaves, McVeigh
supposedly even had a chip implant.

What's your take on this, is it possible that
those men were mind control slaves and can

you give us an idea of how easy (or difficult) it is to create the perfect MC slave and how they are trained and controlled? What are signs or clues that would give away whether these criminals may have been mind controlled?

Svali: I believe strongly that many of these people are people who had MK ULTRA or military training/assassin training that went "bad". In fact, I KNOW a few of those guys were, and if you read up on the cases, there is almost always a mention of Nazi or occult paraphernalia in the home (unless they have covered it up); web sites with occult and Nazi symbolism (such as in the Colorado shootings a couple of years ago at the high school) or other signs pointing to some amount of involvement in a cult or the occult.

Why do I think they have this training? First, because no one just picks up a gun one day and learns how to shoot (and hit their target). Where did these people learn to aim and shoot? Where did they do their target practice, and develop their deadly accuracy in many cases?

When I was a trainer in the Illuminati, there was one command that every trainer learned first when working with their subjects (and assassin training was then mandatory for ALL children, I went through it and do not know of any children in the Illuminati who have not). The command? The "halt" command. This is the FIRST command put in, it freezes the child or teen or adult in place, and is ground in.

Why do trainers learn this code first for the person they work with? Because of the real risk that the person may try to kill them, and the halt code bypasses this. This is a person who has been horrendously abused in atrocious ways from infancy on. This is a person taught since age five to shoot, first with air guns and BB shot, later real guns, and to practice using VR equipment.

This is a person taught in early childhood to kill coldly and emotionlessly on command. This is a person who is told to shoot their brother or sister during a VR exercise, and they believe it is real under hypnotic trance, to test their "obedience". (They actually did this horrible thing to my son, and he cried as he told how anxious he was the next day, and almost died of shock to see his sister alive and well. That was the ONLY way he knew it had been a VR exercise and NOT real).

This is a person with endless rage towards their tormentors and abusers after a lifetime of torture, abuse and rape, who is told to "use their anger" to make them a better marksmen. This is a person told that eliminating the "enemy" and the weak will bring them glory and help "family". Now, if that child or teen or adult is alone and tormented in the daytime, a great anger will build up. This person becomes difficult to control.

At night, I knew trainers (who were sloppy or pushed too hard) who were killed by the person they were working on. It was considered one of the "risks of the job". I was always cautious. All trainers knew that at night a person might get out of control, it always happened some. The person was highly punished for it, locked up for days, tortured, to teach them that it wasn't okay. If the person became very unstable, they might be considered "expendable" and eliminated. Or sent to a state hospital, where no one would believe their "paranoid fantasies" of being taught to assassinate others.

If the brutal and controlling trainers had trouble controlling people and at times were killed by them, then why wouldn't they occasionally lose control in the daytime? It happens, and is quietly covered up (guess how quickly the FBI yanks away incriminating web sites or occult paraphernalia or anything linking the person to an organized occult group?).

People do not suddenly become killers. It is a learned process to overcome the natural horror of killing other human beings, a process begun in earliest childhood by the Illuminati. You have to FORCE a child to kill.

Here is how it is done (how it was done to me):

[1] When the child is 2 years old, place them in a metal cage with electrodes attached. Shock the child severely.

[2] Take the child out, and place a kitten in its hands. Tell the child to wring the kitten's neck. The child will cry and refuse.

[3] Put the child into the cage, and shock them until they are dazed and cannot scream any more.

[4] Take the child out, and tell them again to wring the kitten's neck. This time the child will shake all over, cry, but do it, afraid of the torture. The child will then go into the corner and vomit afterwards, while the adult praises them for "doing such a good job".

This is the first step. The animals get bigger over time, as the child gets older. They will be forced to kill an infant at some point, either a set up or VR, or in reality. They will be taught by age 9 to put together a gun, to aim, and fire on target and on command. They will then practice on realistic manikins. They will then practice on animals. They will then practice on "expendables" or in VR. They will be highly praised if they do well, and tortured if they don't comply.

The older the child or teen, the more advanced the training. By age 15, most children will also be forced to do hand to hand combat in front of spectators (high people who come to watch the "games" much as the ancient gladiators performed). These matches are rarely done to the death, usually until one child goes down. They use every type of weapon imaginable, and learn to fight for their lives. If a child loses a fight, they are heavily punished by their trainer, who loses "face". If they win, they are again praised for being "strong' and adept with weapons. By the time they are 21, they are well trained combat/killing machines with command codes to kill and they have been tested over and over to prove that they WILL obey on command. This is how children in the German Illuminati are brought up, I went through it myself.

Q: Svali, you said earlier that a 'halt' program is one of the first programs installed in children. What exactly does it consist of? Is it just a code word, or a more complicated process?

Svali: Normally, the halt program is a code that freezes the child or adult in their tracks. It is a combination of numbers, such as "354" (not a real one, just similar as an example), or a German word and number combination.

All children will try to hurt their trainers back, it ALWAYS happens, at a very young age. The part of them that tried to do the hurting (usually a protector) will be severely punished, with imprisonment and isolation, or being beaten, or shocked, or a combination to teach them not to do this.

The halt command will then be put in under

hypnosis, while drugged, after extreme trauma. The alter with the command is told to come out INSTANTEOUSLY on hearing it, and to freeze the body with no movement; the person is told that if they fail to do this, many more torture sessions will follow as punishment. It is reinforced frequently over time.

The Illuminati

Exclusive Interview with an Ex-Illuminati Programmer/Trainer

Illuminati Symbols and Clues; Level of Infiltration

Q: 'Yes, tell me more about that (German connection, Masonic temple, the 'institute' and the Baal statue in Canada, please). What are some of the Illuminati trademarks, symbols and clues that are placed throughout society as their signals (other than the pyramid and all-seeing-eye of Horus), intentionally or unintentionally. Do the Illuminati get careless?

A: To completely answer these questions, you

would need my whole biography. I had thought once about writing it, but I doubt many would read it (seriously, this isn't false modesty) and also I really don't believe people will do anything about the Illuminati even if they know. Sorry for the cynicism, but it is based on a lifetime of experience.

The Illuminists don't care who prints this stuff, or if they are "exposed" because they are counting on the majority not believing it, having done a pretty good job with a media blitz campaign (seen any articles in Newsweek or Time lately that addresses this other than as a laughable conspiracy theory? Guess who owns Time-Warner?).

I have heard them laughing about this very thing in leadership meetings five years ago, and I doubt their attitude has changed much since then. If people DID believe this, if action were able to be taken, then I would be very surprised and quite happy.

I'll give you an example. Two years ago, I tried to find a publisher for my book on how the Illuminati program people. I wanted it available for therapists who work with survivors. I couldn't find anyone willing to consider it; they told me it was much too controversial, and "there is no market for this among the general public". Sad, but true.

At the same time, I do believe that God is in control of world history. I have exposed them, and self published my book for free on the web, to let those who work with survivors realize what they have been through. It's hard to help people leaving a group without understanding the traumas both emotional and physical that they have endured.

Okay, now to your questions.

1. The Bruderheist is the ruling council of Germany. It meets in the black forest region, which is considered the center of the earth, and a vortex for psychical/spiritual energy. They are some of the most vicious people I have ever known in my life, and make the Nazis (who they encouraged) look like fun people. They are still there, manipulating people, running banks, and channeling their dirty money to Brussels, Switzerland, and Cairo, Egypt.

2. Canada has a very large Illuminati and Templar Knight community (they are hand in glove groups) that worship ancient deities. The gold or bronze statue of Baal is in a holy

grove on a large private estate between Quebec and Montreal. Since I was only 12 years old when I went there, the details aren't quite as clear. But the ceremonies there were full of people in white gowns, lots of flowers and fruits and votive offerings, singing, then the final sacrifice in the arms of the statue.

3. Illuminati trademarks: these are the most cautionary people on earth. They try to leave absolutely NO tracks. Most of the symbiology can be seen on T.V. or movies, and include: the concept of a military government ruling. These people are very, very militaristic.

The Phoenix: this is one of their highest military and spiritual symbols. If you see a German eagle, too, this is a huge sign. Certain companies will use a phoenix as their logo, especially red on black, or the reverse, this is a huge sign, since the Illuminati use many resuscitation rituals in their training, where the person is brought into a death, or near death state, then "resuscitated" and told that Baal, or some other entity, "gave them life" and they owe their new life to him and the group. Thus, the phoenix is a huge trigger and symbol.

Butterflies and rainbow signs are big triggers

for people who have gone through the Monarch programming (yes, the Illuminists invented Monarch programming with the CIA). Certain types of jewelry are used as triggers. If a person goes online, and plays certain role games (like Ultima) the games are FULL of trigger symbols, such as gem stones. I don't play them but my husband does, and I have told him what the symbols mean. He thinks it's funny since they don't bother him (he isn't Illuminati).

A tiara, or crown with 13 gems, with a diamond in the center, is a symbol of the coming reign of the "chosen one".

Star of David: believe it or not, one of the highest Illuminati religious symbols is a star of David with a circle around it. Called "the great seal of Solomon" it is used at the highest ceremonies to invoke the demonic.

Earth, water, and fire: these three are used in a lot of ceremonies. Check out how many Saturday a.m. cartoons use this concept. You'd be amazed. In fact, "The Fifth Element" movie was based on it.

Greek and Roman mythology and symbols: The Illuminati use a tremendous amount of

Greek and Roman mythology in their programming, and most people will have internal structures with a Roman or Greek temple inside. Lightening bolts, and any symbols from this time will also trigger those with this inside. For more, just pick up any recent Time magazine. Most of the ads are filled with Illuminati symbiology. A picture of a head with a computer inside is another big one, symbolizes delta programming, for example.

Q: Take the lead and tell me about issues you may not have covered in your articles or in this interview.... perhaps some issues I have missed in regards to the New World Order/ global government and such...

A: 1. These people are pedophiles, they abuse and torture small children and teach them under duress to become perpetrators themselves from earliest infancy. This alone means they should be stopped.

They run the porn industry, along with other groups such as the Mafia. They make enormous amounts of money from drug smuggling, gun running, and human slavery (oh, yes, the buying and selling of human beings is alive and well in the 21st century).

They are involved in evil and money making in the extreme. If a profit is being made off of human suffering, you can trace the chain back somewhere to these people.

2. They have money and lawyers that could blast anyone confronting them out of the water.

3. They have infiltrated our government, and the governments of every country in the world, and well as the judicial and legal systems.

4. The media as well.

5. They run our financial institutions.

6. They are ruthless, ambitious, and will not stop at killing those they oppose. They invented MK-Ultra with the help of the CIA. Still want to take them on? Sorry, just letting you know what they are like.

7. They are working towards bringing in a new leader, who will usher in a Luciferian reign of joy, prosperity, and rewards to the faithful. Almost an Elyssian type paradise. Of course, the brutality would continue, and those who oppose his reign are to be hunted

down and converted or destroyed, but the followers will be so happy and content that they believe these holdouts will want to come over to their side. Sounds unbelievable, but true.

Also, people will have new jobs, and leadership positions in this new order, since the Illuminati believe that their children are the brightest and best (remember that lifetime of training and teaching?) and will be the intellectual elite who will rule over the unintelligent, or "less fit". These people really, truly believe this, and almost worship Plato's ideal Republic as their blue print for the new order.

Now, the other side of the picture.

1. They are arrogant, and this could be their downfall. They view the common man as "sheep" with no intelligence. They are full of pride, believe they are invulnerable and that any press about them is the equivalent of a gnat to be swatted. Arrogant people make mistakes, and they are becoming more blatant and open in recent years.

2. They believe they can overcome God, which

is a huge mistake. God can stay the hand of history, and has so far, in the hope that more from this group will get out, because He is merciful.

3. Most of them are wounded, abused victims, who don't realize that it is possible to leave the group. There is a lot of discontent in the ranks, and there would be a mass exodus if the members believed it were really possible to get out (and live). Many of the trainers I knew (I know, wicked, torturing pedophiles) were NOT happy with what they did. They would whisper quietly, or give a look, to show that they disagreed with what they had to do. They would resignedly do their jobs, in the hope of advancement.

Know what one of the biggest carrots offered to those who advance up in the group is? That you don't have to hurt people anymore, and that you can't be abused (it's true: only those higher than you in the group can abuse you, so everyone wants to move up, where the pool of candidates becomes smaller). Of course, people can choose to abuse anyone beneath them, and that motivates some (but not all!) to move up.

4. As more survivors leave, therapists and

churches and support people are becoming more aware of the sophisticated mind control techniques used to control members. They are learning to undo it.

5. Prayer can overcome the greatest evil, and my greatest hope is that those I once knew in this group, including the heads and those who hurt me at times, would get out. That they could know that, yes, it is truly possible to leave.

Q: I have seen Clinton do this hand sign on a few occasion, and now Prince William as well. Any hidden meaning?

A: That is an old, well known greeting of one Satanist to another. Usually, the Illuminists are a lot more subtle and don't do that publicly.

CHAPTER SIXTEEN

The Illuminati

Exclusive Interview with an Ex-Illuminati
Programmer/Trainer

The Top of the Pyramid

Q: Svali, a very important question I'm sure
all our readers are asking themselves is, who
heads the Illuminati? Who is the top of the
pyramid?

A: Hooboy! Where do I start with this? First, it
depends on what level. I would like to draw up
a little map of the Illuminati from my
memories (which are NOT FOND) of being
part of this group. I will also try to fill in some
names, but I want to be cautious. If I name too
many names, I could draw some nasty fire
from people in the group. Here it goes:

I will be doing an upside down pyramid, to

show the Illuminati structure, NOT to trigger people (I know the Illuminati use lots of pyramids) but because this is how they have their hierarchy set up:

Level One: Local level: (anytown, USA)

Sister group   sister group   sister group   sister group   sister group

There will be between ten and thirty sister groups in most metropolitan areas, dependent on the size of the city. The larger the city, the more sister groups. There are Illuminati groups in EVERY major city in the US and Europe. This first level is what is known as the "anarchical" or "low level". It is what most people reporting ritual abuse discuss: a high priest and priestess preside over each group, which also contains a group of two to four trainers, and others with jobs. The sister groups unite on rare occasions, are aware of each other, but each one is fairly independent, and reports only to their leadership council.

Level Two: Metropolitan leadership council:

This is what the local leadership council over these groups will look like. It will also cover scattered groups in outlying rural areas.

Baalim (head) (1), assistants to the head (2) administrators over finances and day to day happenings (4), head trainers (oversee and teach other trainers) (6).

The total: 13 members

The Baalim and his two assistants report to:

REGIONAL LEADERSHIP COUNCIL

The United States has been divided into seven different regions geographically. Each region has a 13 member leadership council that coordinates with the local leadership councils (are you getting the idea by now? The Illuminati are set up a lot like "Amway" or any other well-organized business enterprise with a flowchart of accountability for each member). This council will look something like this:

Head of council (1), Military (2 seats), Spiritual (2 seats), Scholarship (2 seats), Finances (2 seats), Training (2 seats), Sciences (2 seats).

Total: 13 members

The regional councils will represent the different areas of interest and knowledge that the Illuminati pursue. The membership will change over time as members are promoted or demoted.

The seven regional councils each have a leader as noted above, who reports to the:

National Council (The nations in Europe also have National Councils, Mexico and Canada do as well, as does the Soviet Republic and China).

The national council will look much like the one above, with this difference; these are influential bankers with OLD money such as: The Rockefellers, the Mellon family, the Carnegie family, the Rothschild family etc. I know I shouldn't name names, but I will.

The heads of the National councils report to:

The Supreme World Council.

This council is already set up as a prototype of the one that will rule when the NWO comes into being. It meets on a regular basis to discuss finances, direction, policy, etc. and to problem-solve difficulties that come up. Once again, these leaders are heads in the financial world, OLD banking money. The Rothschild family in England, and in France, have ruling seats. A descendant of the Hapsburg dynasty has a generational seat. A descendant of the ruling families of England and France have a generational seat. The Rockefeller family in the US holds a seat.

This is one reason that the Illuminati have been pretty "untouchable" over the years. The ruling members are very, very, very wealthy and powerful. I hope this information is helpful. How do I know this? I was on a local leadership council (a head trainer), but I talked to those on regional. Also, every Illuminati child is taught who their "leaders" are, and told to take an oath of allegiance to them and the "New Order to come".

Q: To what degree is the European royalty involved, what is their real pecking order and power structure and what is their U.S.-U.K. relationship in terms of financial/political/cult power. Is the Monarchy still running the show?

A: This is hard to answer, but I'll try. The Illuminati leadership state that they are descended from royal bloodlines, as well as unbroken occult heritage.

See, there were two definitions of "royalty" used. Open royalty that is currently seen now, and "hidden royalty" of royal lineage and extreme occult power. Sometimes the two were concurrent, such as with the Prince of Wales.

I never thought of which country/line held the most power, since I was just a peon busily doing my job. But my understanding was: The Hanoverian / Hapsburg descendants rule in Germany over the Bruderheist. They are considered one of the strongest lines for occult as well. The British line is just under them, with the royal family. Definitely, they rule the UK branch under the Rothschilds in the occult realm, even though parliament rules the country openly.

In France, again, descendants of the royal families are also in power in the occult realm, but the French Rothschilds hold the reigns over all or them. The U.S. is considered lower, and younger, than the European branches. This is why the children of leaders are ALWAYS sent to Europe for part of their training; the education is considered better and the U.S. families want to renew their affiliation with the European forebears.

Germany, France, and the UK form a triumvirate that rules in the European cult. The USSR is considered important, and has the strongest military groups. The USSR has been promised fourth position in the New World Order, BEFORE the role the U.S. would have, because the USSR has been more helpful and cooperative over the years with furthering the agenda.

The descendants of the former ruling families there are also involved in the occult leadership, along with the newer ones. There is no Marxism in the cult. China will be ranked after the USSR, then the U.S. But a lot of the current U.S. leadership will be in Europe when the change occurs, and many have homes there. They will be "changing nationalities" overnight, as it were. This is the little that I do remember. Wish I had been a better student of this stuff, but I was too busy trying to stay alive when I was in it.

Illuminati Proof - Vulnerabilities

Q: Svali, have you ever come forward publicly with that story, or is this the first time?

A: I have never gone into the demonic aspects much, because it is so controversial (i.e. your question below!). I have shared this before with my husband, my therapist, and a close friend. I'm not really a "public" person, I've only posted some articles at Suite101.com, to help others who are trying to get out of the cult.

I hate sensationalizing stuff, personally, because it can detract from the real problem; children are being hurt and abused, and the abuse needs to stop. Call it demons, aliens, or whatever, there are evil men (and women) using small children and profiting from their pain. That is why I have spoken out against this group.

Q: I am certain that a lot of readers will say 'Come on, now I know this is just sci-fi, how can this be real?!' and would want to see some proof or evidence to that. What would you say to them?

I would say "go to a ritual, you will see plenty"

except that I don't want ANYONE to ever see or be near that type of evil. Spiritual realities don't leave physical marks, but I think it is interesting that throughout recorded history, mankind has written about these type of phenomena.

Could all of our recorded histories be false? Could mankind be a pathological liar throughout the centuries in this area? If a person visits Africa, they will also hear accounts of shape shifting done by the occult, and there, they DON'T dissociate, so you can interview people who have seen it while fully conscious.

In South America, and Asia, this also occurs. How could a world-wide phenomena be made up by groups that had no previous contact with each other?

Does the demonic leave a trail, a mark that I can point to? No. But does it leave an indelible impression on those that have witnessed it? Yes, and even in pre-medieval times, this type of stuff was recorded.

I didn't take videos or snapshots of this stuff happening, so a person has to decide whether they believe it or not based on oral testimony.

I don't really care. I know what I saw.

Q: Also, to wrap this interview up for now, what do you see as the Illuminati's Achilles Heel, their vulnerability? Is there any way to stop them, and a way for humanity to move on and say 'It is finished!'?

At the moment it seems hopeless, sort of like having your fingers in a Chinese finger trap, - you know what I'm talking about - with no way out.

A: 1. Their arrogance (I think I mentioned this before) is their weakness. These people think they are untouchable, and this could make them careless.

2. If by a miracle, enough people took this SERIOUSLY and started organizing in some way to stop the Illuminati take over, with prayer and God's guidance, perhaps they could be stopped. I hope so, with all of my heart.

3. Stopping pornography and child prostitution and drug smuggling and gun running would take out a huge chunk of their profits. Maybe they would slow down. But honestly, stopping the above would be as

difficult as stopping the group.

4. To be honest, I don't know what could really stop them. I have written about this group to try and expose them, I have gone to the police several times, given videotaped testimony against them in a court case (the interview was with 5 lawyers and took 3 hours), knowing that my ex-head trainer would be seeing a copy of the video (I thought about smiling and waving and saying "hi Jonathan", but then decided that might be going a little too far).

I have encouraged others in getting out, and helped a few survivors find safe housing and a way to stay out. I guess each person has to do their best in fighting these people, in the way they feel led to. My skills tend to be in writing, so I am using them.

Q: If you have any last comments or think there are some areas we have not touched or topics you would like to take us to, please feel free to share those.

A: If anyone has heard the sobs of a child when it has been used brutally by adults, or the screams of a child psychologically terrorized, they would do anything they could to stop this abuse.

There are children as young as three and four being used in pornographic films, beaten black and blue if they refuse to comply. There are toddlers being forced to watch brutalities, then given a stick and told to go over and hit the victim themselves, or they will be beaten. The child hesitates, it doesn't want to, and the adults hit the child, until the child goes, tears streaming down its face, and unwillingly does what the adults tell it. This is cruelty beyond belief.

To see a slightly older child with an electric dog collar around its neck, shocked when it tries to "escape" and treated as an animal, to the laughter of the adults and older children around it, and the child goes over to a bush and vomits from fear and self-loathing.

These are the pictures that any survivor of the Illuminati holds in their heart, and these are the reasons I will write and write about them to expose them, and why my heartfelt prayer is that they can be stopped. I wish I were making this up, but I'm not. I wish I didn't have these pictures engraved in my memory, but I do.

Q: Svali, would you be willing to answer readers' questions or feedback, in form of some future article? I think there may be some questions coming in for you at some point, probably to cover some details about your story.

A: I would prefer that they send their questions to you, and then you forward them, if possible. I don't want to get a lot of "hate mail" because I am writing about a topic that is controversial and politically incorrect to talk about.

I'm sure there will be those who say, "oh, she just wants attention". Well, I get plenty of attention at the classes I teach, with a room full of students, and lots more fun besides. I get attention seeing my NON abuse articles in print, and make money besides (which I don't when I write about this).

No, I want to expose these people; that's my motivation. Some will believe what I am writing, others won't. That's fine with me. If they feel the need to vent their disbelief, that's fine, as long as I don't get lots of cuss words, or people saying I'm stupid (oh, yes, I get letters like that at times) or uneducated.

Sorry, none of the above is true. I have 2 university degrees. I had to, I was told to by the cult. They don't let stupid people lead.

Oh, and HJ, I won't just disappear on you or recant anything I wrote. You can email me anytime with questions, and I will delightedly expose what SOBs this group is composed of. Oops, that doesn't sound Christian there, but God appreciates honesty, doesn't He? I'm only accurately describing them. I'm still working on forgiveness, as you can see...

Q: Svali, I'm grateful you took the time to share those experiences with us, which I'm sure was neither easy nor pleasant. I wish you all the best, for you and your family. Perhaps more people will read this, and pass this article on to others. Maybe we can stop all of this shocking brutality, child abuse, the Illuminati someday. It's never too late. Thank your very much for this interview, Svali.

With the writing and compiling of this book, I am passing Svali's message on to you, the reader. The only weapons we have against this evilarchy is information and the hope and prayer that God will protect us as we try to expose this evil organization. Information is truly a weapon. The more people who become aware of the Illuminati Luciferian Agenda, the better chance we have of stopping this blight on humanity. There are other researchers and writers that have the courage to write against the Iluminati. I mention a few here in hopes that you will read their books and gain more knowledge of the enemy. Knowledge is power. Here are a few writers I hope you will gain knowledge from: Alex Jones, David Icke, Texe Marrs, the late Bill Cooper's writings and videos. Out there somewhere is a person with enough knowledge and courage to build a workable plan to combat the Illuminati Luciferian Agenda of global enslavement.

Robert Greyeagle

August 2012